No
Reservations
Required

No Reservations Required

Easy Manageable Recipes
Culinary Creations that Rival the Best of Restaurants

Bev & John Shaffer

The Wooster Book Company
Wooster Ohio • 2003

The Wooster Book Company
where minds and imaginations meet

205 West Liberty Street
Wooster Ohio • 44691
www. woosterbook.com
800-WUBOOK-1

1-59098-166-9

Library of Congress Cataloging-in-Publication Data

Shaffer, Bev, 1951–
No reservations required / Bev & John Shaffer.
p.   cm.
ISBN 1-59098-166-9 (alk. paper) ∞
1. Cookery, American. 2. Cookery, International. I. Shaffer, John, 1937– II. Title

TX715.S1465 2001
641.5973 – dc21   2001046828

Dedications

From Bev: To my Mom, Olga (affectionately known as "The Gyps"), who taught me to love to cook. Thanks, Mom!

From John: To my Mother, Jane, whose love and encouragement were always an inspiration.

No Reservations Required

Table of *Contents*

Acknowledgements

Thanks to: David Wiesenberg and the good people at The Wooster Book Company for their encouragement and guidance; Rick Zaidan of Zaidan Photography for the back cover photo; and to our students and friends for never letting up on the pressure of "How's the book coming?"

Introduction

People talk about a passion for cooking...it definitely has been for us.

The greatest joy (aside from the pure pleasure of cooking itself and sharing the results with family and friends) has been the teaching of others.

For years in our own cooking school we have been very grateful for our dedicated following of students and the thanks we have received from them for this sharing...how rewarding and fulfilling this continues to be.

It is in this spirit we pass on to the readers of this book our creations and the tips and techniques to make their preparation and presentation easier.

And where have these creations come from, since we're constantly looking for new recipes? Some have come as middle-of-the-night inspirations, some are our own updates on the classics, and some are family heirlooms or have been shared by friends, while others are gleaned from visits to restaurants. No matter what the origin, by the time we've added our own twists, techniques and tastes and tested! tested! tested! they become our signature recipes.

Just a few observations...perhaps you lack the knowledge to cook, e.g. you're kitchen illiterate! Give yourself a pep talk with these few preachy but basic words:

- *Think of cooking as fun, not work ("fun cooking" is not an oxymoron)*

- *Think of cooking as recreation*

- *No one is too busy to cook – you simply need to make it a priority*

- *Be realistic about your skill level...novice cooks should begin with easy recipes to gain and foster confidence in the kitchen...easy, manageable recipes do exist in this book just waiting for you.*

Enjoy preparing these recipes at home – creations that will rival (or exceed) the best of restaurants.

And remember to savor the flavors!

Bev & John

Bev & John

Observations

Bev talks:

While this book was in its manuscript stage, people would ask me what the title was and how it came about.

Think about it – so many of us did not learn to cook at our mother's (or father's) side. Many of you might not even cook, or to you cooking is basically putting together on a plate some purchased food – but you do eat out frequently (hopefully, some of you even dine out!).

So, your tastes have become too sophisticated – and you've come around to cooking at home because:

- You're sick of eating out!
- You need some new, creative recipes!
- You want the satisfaction of creating something delicious from scratch!
- You're about to entertain and you're morbidly curious about how it feels to share what you've created with others!

GRAB THIS BOOK! Sophisticated yet simple recipes that will rival even the best take out food – tested and taught – and picked by our students as some of their favorites.

As an aside: I always try to instill the thought that a recipe is a license to create and experiment by substituting ingredients and flavors. However, if you're new to cooking don't be intimidated by your kitchen or these recipes, and for best success, try the recipe as stated before you begin substitutions and changes of your own.

When developing and writing recipes, we concentrate on a few seemingly obvious and very basic things.

Taste! Taste! Taste! When we develop a recipe, taste is always the number one consideration. Our teaching philosophy has always been (sing along with us, children): #1 in importance is an easy to follow, tested recipe; #2 is quality ingredients (the object of these two is to create the best taste possible – even though we eat with our eyes first and presentation is important, eventually we eat with our mouths!); and #3 is everything else – which includes technique and to a lesser degree equipment.

One final note: cook with the seasons (forget asparagus and red raspberries in February and instead enjoy citrus and greens) – think local and seasonal.

Enjoy playing with your food!

Tips & Techniques

John talks:

About the seemingly obvious and very basic. (Oh, don't worry – Bev added her remarks too!)

Good Equipment (not to be confused with Bad Equipment or "don't waste your money on that, honey!"): We have our favorites – but remember, good equipment doesn't automatically make you a better cook, it simply makes cooking and usually clean up easier. The more experienced cook you are the more you appreciate quality equipment. As an example, quality in a saucepan will cause it to heat so evenly that you can cook delicate ingredients on a low heat without fear of "hot spots" and burning.

A sharp peeler or quality garlic press will run circles around ones of poorer quality – and some of those cheaper ones simply don't work.

Stainless steel is a fine metal for saucepans because stainless steel doesn't interact with acidic foods such as tomatoes. However, by itself stainless steel is a poor conductor of heat; therefore, it needs the addition of a thick layer of copper or aluminum across the bottom and possibly up the sides to distribute the heat evenly and avoid the already mentioned "hot spots."

Quality cutlery and cookware are the most basic and probably the most important tools (or to us the toys). You don't have to have more than three or four of each in order to have a well-equipped kitchen.

In the case of knives, a 3" parer, an 8" chef's knife and an 8" or 10" slicing knife of high quality will do nicely. (Fourth would be the Wusthoff Trident tomato knife.)

In cookware, two heavy saucepans, 1-1/2 quart and 3-1/2 quart, a 10" or 12" skillet (nonstick is handy if you get one that's guaranteed for life against pitting and peeling) and a French (Dutch) oven, about 5-quart size, for soups and stews.

On Our Soapbox: With heavy quality cookware you will seldom need to turn the heat above medium. Be sure to follow the manufacturer's recommendations for care. Always wash by hand! And, with cutlery, use the same care recommendations. Do not soak your knives or leave them in the sink (too dangerous! the stuff horror movies are made of!) and wash by hand. Buy forged high carbon stainless steel knives or all carbon steel.

Also, buy a steel and hone your knives frequently. Knives occasionally need to be sharpened in addition to honing. (Do not – and we'll find you if you do – use the grinding wheel on the back of your can opener.)

Honing doesn't take metal off and should be done almost every time you use your knife. However, when honing doesn't get your knife sharp it's time to actually sharpen the knife. Sharpening takes metal off the blade while it realigns the edge, so do this sparingly (if you want to have any metal left on your knife) – once or twice per year usually is enough for normal home use.

Sharpening requires a different tool other than the steel – some of our favorites are:
- Chef's Choice (EdgeCraft) electric knife sharpener
- The Diamond Vee or Diamond Steel by DMT

Once you get used to this honing and sharpening procedure, your knives will be sharp. You won't believe how much easier a sharp knife makes the task of slicing, dicing and chopping.

A knife block near your prep area is a good idea. It keeps the edges protected from dulling and a slot for a steel makes it handy for a quick honing. (Knife blocks that have horizontal slots are easiest on the knife edge.)

Our favorite manufacturers and lines:

Cutlery
- Wusthoff Trident (professional line, forged)
- LamsonSharp (wood handle, forged)
- Sabatier (all carbon, forged)

Cookware
- Berndes (wood handle, nonstick)
- Bourgeat (stainless with aluminum base)
- All Clad (LTD)
- Le Creuset (porcelain-covered cast iron/ French ovens, all sizes)

Bev's comments: These cookware lines are on our kitchen pot racks. They are a dream to cook with and clean up and I grab a variety and assortment of these pieces again and again. Other "toys" that make a difference because of ease of use:

Peeler: Kuhn Rikon all carbon steel, plastic color handle (you won't believe how sharp a peeler can be!)

Electric Stand Mixer: KitchenAid KSM90

Food Processor: KitchenTools by Black & Decker or Cuisinart

Parchment Paper: excellent to line cookie sheets in place of greasing; great for pouch cooking (en papillote) for fish and other foods

Garlic Press: Susi by Zyliss (you don't need to peel the garlic cloves when you use this beauty!)

Mortar and Pestle: great for grinding dried herbs and seeds (marble or porcelain)

Timers: electronic triple timer

Wooden Spoons: multiple sizes, buy quality cherry or French beech

Wooden Bowls: medium size for chopping with a mezzaluna or for mixing and serving

Twine: French is best; use on rolled roasts, stuffing poultry, flank steak rolls, tying on your finger so you won't forget something, and many other uses – easy to use and remove after cooking

Pepper Mills: A good pepper mill is indispensable for use in the kitchen as well as at the table. There is no substitute for freshly ground pepper. We like to have two pepper mills on hand, one for white peppercorns and one for black. Stainless grinding mechanisms are important. Some of our favorite brands: Peugeot and William Bounds.

Kitchen Shears: Joyce Chen (original design); stays sharp; buy an extra pair for gardening

French Porcelain Baking Dishes: quality equals ease of clean up; great serving dishes (Emile Henry brand is superb)

Strawberry Huller (stainless): hasn't changed since Grandma Shaffer used it more than 50 years ago – still the easiest way to hull strawberries – easier on fingernails, saves more of the berry

Instant Read Thermometer: Taylor digital – the safest and easiest way to check the doneness of meats, bread, etc. Also used to check liquid for proofing yeast when making breads.

Whisk: A must in a well-equipped kitchen. One medium-size or one small and one large stainless steel with comfortable handle (wood or rubber handle).

Zester: Lemon zest stripped with a lemon zester and finely chopped with your chef's knife has a multitude of uses and adds superior flavor to everything from a fruit salad dressing to desserts. Don't skimp; buy the best if you want it sharp (or buy a Microplane zester/grater).

Shrimp Deveiner: The one piece, simple metal design works best. Why shell and devein shrimp yourself? Taste! Taste! Taste! As soon a shrimp is shelled it begins to dry out and loose flavor (even if frozen immediately). So, shell them yourself and don't overcook them. You will notice the difference in flavor and texture. Deveining is for the top vein (called the sand vein – opposite the little legs or swimmerets). This vein should be removed to eliminate any possible gritty taste from sand.

Other handy "toys": a triple mesh stainless steel cone strainer; stainless steel graters, one flat hand-size, the other a four-sided grater; skimmers, one wire and one mesh; a colander and a salad spinner; mushroom brush to clean (never wash or they absorb the water and become slimy!) your fresh mushrooms as soon as you get them home from the store, then put them into a paper bag and refrigerate; an egg separator.

Tips: One of the best tips we can give you is to learn how to tell when things are done cooking. Many times the suggested time in a recipe is an estimate because many factors can effect the amount of time a recipe takes to cook something. (One of the biggest mistakes people make in baking cakes and in cooking chicken and seafood is overcooking it until it's dry!) Now don't give up on us – follow this.

Some of the factors are:

- Ovens are notoriously off temperature by 25 to 50 degrees
  (use an oven thermometer to get an accurate reading).
- The pan used (heat conductivity differs widely by type of material,
  i.e. stainless, glass, aluminum).
- Temperature of the pan and the ingredients when cooking begins
  (were the ingredients at room temperature or directly from the refrigerator?).
- And blah, blah, blah.

The important point is that knowing how to tell when your recipe is done is not completely by the clock.

Recipes will tell you what to look for or how to recognize these doneness signs.

Some of the tools that will help:

- A timer (or 3) to let you know when to check for doneness
- An instant read thermometer to check internal temperature
- Toothpick or cake tester
- Your finger (i.e. to check springiness of a cake) and
  to lick the batter before the cake goes in
- Fork to check fish for flakiness
- Fork to check crispness of vegetables

A few other miscellaneous tips:

To "seed" a tomato when it is called for in a recipe, core the tomato (a melon baller works great for this task), slice it in half vertically and squeeze under running water.

To "seed" a pepper, slice off top and bottom then slice down sides leaving core with seeds attached. Remove and discard core and seeds.

Measure for Measure: To bake successfully, you must measure ingredients exactly. Have two kinds of measuring cups: dry, with flushed rim, comes in sets (usually 1/4, 1/3, 1/2 and 1 cup), and liquid, with a lipped cup for pouring, with levels marked on the side. Measuring spoons are also essential.

For flour and sugar: Use a dry measuring cup in the size you need, fill, heaping slightly. Run a knife across top to level off. For liquids: Use a liquid measuring cup, filling to desired level. For brown sugar: Use a dry measuring cup, pack down, level off excess with knife.

To store garlic: the two best ways – in a clay covered container with holes for ventilation, kept away from heat and direct sunlight; peeled cloves in a jar with a tightly closed lid (a canning jar works well for this) and stored in the refrigerator.

Words to Eat By...

Only dull people are brilliant at breakfast.
— Oscar Wilde, Anglo-Irish playwright and critic

(To John) The most dangerous food a man can eat is wedding cake.
— American proverb

I did toy with the idea of doing a cookbook . . . The recipes were to be the routine ones: how to make dry toast, instant coffee, hearts of lettuce and brownies. But as an added attraction, at no extra charge, my idea was to put a fried egg on the cover. I think a lot of people who hate literature but love fried eggs would buy it if the price was right.
— Groucho Marx, American comedian and author

For those who love it, cooking is at once child's play and adult joy. And cooking done with care is an act of love.
— Craig Claiborne, American food writer

If you can't stand the heat, get out of the kitchen.
— Harry S. Truman, thirty third President of the United States

When life gives you lemons, make lemonade.
— Anonymous

The so-called nouvelle cuisine usually means
not enough on your plate and too much on your bill.
— Paul Bocuse, French chef

What is patriotism but the love of good things
we ate in our childhood?
— Lin Yutang, Chinese American author

A woman is like a tea bag -
only in hot water do you realize how strong she is.
— Nancy Reagan, American First Lady

Recipes are traditions, not just random words of ingredients.
— Anonymous

Cuisine is when things taste like themselves.
— Curnonsky, French gastronome, author and editor

This recipe is certainly silly. It says to separate eggs,
but it doesn't say how far to separate them.
— Gracie Allen, American actress and comedian

Entertaining with *Pizzazz* (Appetizers, Dips, Salsas and Spreads)

- Chinese Spare Ribs

- Drunken Shrimp with Salsa Dip

- Balsamic Wings

- Cheese Shortbread

- Zesty Tomato Cheese Fondue

- Baked Goat Cheese with Crumbs

- Cranberry Brie

- Veggie Nachos

- Classic Tomato Salsa

- Mango Salsa and Wonton Chips

- Corn and Black Bean Salsa

- "Party Hats" with Smoked Salmon and Edible Confetti

- Scallion Dill Dip

- Yogurt Cheese

Words to Eat By

The hostess must be like the duck –
calm and unruffled on the surface,
and paddling like hell underneath.
— *Anonymous*

All good cooks learn something
new every day.
— *Julia Child*

Shake and shake
The catsup bottle.
None will come
And then a lot'll.
— *Richard Armour*

Feel that happy, mouthfilling wow?
Taste that gimme-some-more-of-that,
boy-that's-great flavor?
That's salsa?
That's musica for your mouth!
— *Reed Hearon*

Notes from Bev

Appetizers, Dips, Salsas, Spreads

An appetizer party is one of our favorite ways to entertain. We love the mobility, informality and, honestly, the appetizers! So much can be done ahead, and with a varied assortment of appetizers, dips, salsas and spreads your guests can make a meal of it.

A few notes on party planning … we all want blueprints, accurate calculations of how many pieces per person to make and serve. While we can offer some guidelines from our catering experience, remember they are simply that – guidelines. After all, do we know if Jake is still on that high carb diet, or if Melissa is going to eat enough for several people again? You get the idea.

In general, for a 2-to-3 hour party you should plan on two of each kind of bite-size appetizers per person. For twenty people, serve 2 to 3 kinds of cold appetizers and 3 to 4 kinds of hot (one should be low in fat and preferably vegetarian).

Above all, when it's party time, never panic! Enjoy!

Chinese Spare Ribs

Ingredients:

1/2 cup soy sauce

1/2 cup plum jelly, jam or preserves

2 1/2 Tablespoons dry sherry

2 cloves garlic, pressed

1 1/2 teaspoons Five Spice Powder

2 pounds pork spare ribs, cut into 1-1/2 inch long pieces

In a 2-quart saucepan, combine the soy sauce, plum jelly, sherry, garlic and Five Spice Powder. Heat and stir until plum jelly is melted; cool.

Place ribs in a heavy-duty plastic bag in a baking dish. Pour marinade into bag. Squeeze out any excess air in the bag, then seal. Marinate 2 to 3 hours in the refrigerator, turning bag several times.

Heat oven to 425F. Remove spareribs from plastic bag; reserve marinade.

Place ribs, meaty side down, in a shallow, foil lined pan; cover. Bake for 30 minutes.

Uncover; carefully drain fat from spareribs. Turn meaty side up.

Reduce heat to 350F. Brush spareribs with marinade. Bake at 350F for 30 minutes. Drain fat if necessary. Brush again with marinade. Bake an additional 15 minutes or until ribs are tender.

Serves 4 to 6

Cook's notes from Bev and John

Have the butcher at your meat market or meat department cut ribs across bones to form small riblets.

Don't skip lining the pan with foil – it makes clean up much easier!

13

Drunken Shrimp with Salsa Dip

Use some of our Classic Tomato Salsa for this recipe.

Shrimp:

36 ounces beer (not "lite")

1/4 cup lemon or lime juice

zest of **1** lemon

2 teaspoons **whole black peppercorns**

3 cloves garlic, skin removed then sliced

2 pounds shrimp, shelled and deveined

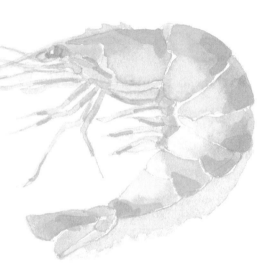

Combine beer, juice, zest, peppercorns and garlic in a 6 to 8 quart saucepan. Bring to a boil.

Reduce heat; cover and simmer 8 minutes.

Add shrimp. Cover and simmer 5 minutes or just until shrimp turns pink. Drain. Cover and refrigerate until thoroughly chilled and ready to serve with the Salsa Dip.

Serves 6+

Salsa Dip:

8 ounces sour cream, regular or nonfat

3/4 cup salsa, mild or hot

Combine sour cream and salsa; mix well. Cover and refrigerate at least 1 hour to blend flavors.

Balsamic Wings

The rich, sweet balsamic vinegar marinade caramelizes to form a crisp glaze on these wings as they cook.

Ingredients:

2 pounds chicken wings
2/3 cup balsamic vinegar
1 cup sweet onion slices

In a large bowl, combine chicken wings, vinegar and onions. Toss well to coat the wings.

Cover the bowl, refrigerate, and let the wings marinate overnight. Stir occasionally.

Heat oven to 450F. Lift the wings out of the marinade and place on a baking sheet in a single layer.

Bake the wings until crisp and deep brown, about 25 minutes. Serve hot or at room temperature.

Serves 4 to 6

Cheese Shortbread

Ingredients:

1 1/4 cups unbleached, all purpose flour

1/2 teaspoon sweet Hungarian paprika

1/8 teaspoon freshly ground white pepper

1/4 teaspoon dry mustard

1/2 cup unsalted butter, room temperature

2 cups shredded sharp cheddar or colby cheese, room temperature

1/2 cup firmly chopped walnuts or pecans

Heat oven to 375F.

Stir together flour, paprika, pepper and mustard
in a bowl; set aside.

Beat together butter and shredded cheese in a large bowl until well blended.
Beat in as much of the flour as you can with the mixer. Stir in any remaining flour by hand.

Place dough on an ungreased baking sheet and pat it into a 12x7 inch rectangle.
Sprinkle with nuts. Press nuts gently into the dough. Cut into 2x1 inch pieces.
Do not separate.

Bake 15 to 18 minutes or until lightly browned. Recut shortbread rectangles
to separate.

Cool on a wire rack. Store in refrigerator or freezer.

Makes about 42 pieces

Zesty *Tomato* Cheese Fondue

This is unbelievably good - if you love the taste of a cheesy pizza, this is for you!

Ingredients:

1 cup finely chopped onion

1 clove garlic, pressed

2 Tablespoons unsalted butter

14.5 ounce can stewed tomatoes

1/2 teaspoon dried basil

1/4 teaspoon dried oregano

1/4 teaspoon ground black pepper

2 cups shredded sharp cheddar cheese

1/3 cup grated Parmesan cheese

1 Tablespoon cornstarch

In a 2-quart saucepan over medium heat, cook onion and garlic in butter until golden.

In bowl, break apart stewed tomatoes (use a fork and knife or a potato masher).
To the saucepan, add tomatoes and their liquid, basil, oregano and pepper. Heat to a simmer.

Meanwhile, combine cheddar, Parmesan and cornstarch in a bowl.

Reduce heat to low and add cheese mixture, 1 cup at a time. Stir until cheeses are melted and blended. Transfer to a chafing dish or leave in the saucepan and keep warm over a hot plate or other heat source (not too hot or it will scorch and burn!).

Serve with wedges of French or Italian bread.

Serves 1 (it's that good) or up to 4

pizzazz

17

Baked *Goat* Cheese with Crumbs

Ingredients:

1/2 cup extra virgin olive oil

1 teaspoon dried thyme

1 bay leaf, crumbled

8 ounce log soft mild goat cheese
(such as Montrachet), cut into 1/2-inch thick rounds

1 cup fresh white bread crumbs, toasted

3 Tablespoons balsamic vinegar

4 to 6 cups assorted salad greens

Salt and Pepper to taste

Combine oil, thyme and bay in small bowl.

Arrange cheese rounds in a single layer in a baking dish.
Pour oil mixture over cheese. Carefully lift and turn cheese to coat.
Cover and refrigerate several hours or up to overnight.

Heat oven to 450F. Line baking sheet with parchment paper. Place bread crumbs in shallow pie plate or cake pan.

Remove cheese from oil; reserve oil. Coat each round with crumbs.

Arrange cheese on prepared baking sheet. Bake until lightly bubbling and golden, about 5 minutes.

Whisk vinegar into reserved oil mixture. Season with salt and pepper, as desired. Place greens in salad bowl and toss with enough vinaigrette to coat lightly.

Place salad greens on individual plates then top with hot cheese rounds and serve.

Serves 2 to 4

Cook's notes from Bev and John
This also works well with infused olive oils,
a garlic or lemon perhaps.

Cranberry Brie

Cranberry Mixture:

3 cups fresh or frozen cranberries

3/4 cup firmly packed light brown sugar

1/3 cup dried cranberries

1/8 teaspoon freshly ground nutmeg

1/8 teaspoon ground allspice

1/4 teaspoon ground cinnamon

1/8 teaspoon ground cloves

1/8 teaspoon ground ginger

zest of **1** lemon

Cheese:

large wheel of Brie cheese
(about 8 inches in diameter)

assorted crackers
pears, cored and sliced
apples, cored and sliced

Combine cranberries, brown sugar, dried cranberries, nutmeg, allspice, cinnamon, cloves, ginger and lemon zest in a 4-quart saucepan. Cook over medium heat until most of the cranberries pop, stirring frequently. Cool to room temperature.

Heat oven to 300F.

Using a sharp knife, cut circle in top rind of cheese, leaving 1/2 inch border of rind. Carefully remove center circle of rind from cheese. Do not cut through side rind.

Place cheese in a round baking dish or on a cookie sheet lined with foil. Spread cranberry mixture over top.

Bake cheese until soft, about 12 minutes. Set cheese on a large platter. Surround with crackers, apple and pear slices. Serve warm or at room temperature.

Serves 6+

Cook's notes from Bev and John
Toss apple and pear slices lightly with fresh lemon juice
and they won't brown as quickly on your serving platter.

Veggie *Nachos*

This is a delicious quick and easy recipe using cupboard staples you probably have on hand.

Ingredients:

1 medium zucchini (about 8 inches long), sliced 1/4 inch to 1/2 inch thick

1/8 teaspoon onion powder

1/8 teaspoon dried basil leaves, crumbled

1/2 cup shredded mozzarella cheese

1/4 cup coarsely chopped pepperoni

2 teaspoons grated Parmesan cheese

Heat oven to 350F.

Arrange zucchini slices on a 10 inch pie plate.

Sprinkle with onion powder and basil. Top with mozzarella cheese, pepperoni and Parmesan cheese.

Bake for 10 minutes or until cheese is melted.

Serves 1 to 2

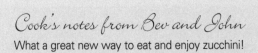

Cook's notes from Bev and John
What a great new way to eat and enjoy zucchini!

Classic Tomato Salsa

If you've never made your own salsa, you're in for a treat!

Ingredients:

2 1/2 cups tomatoes, peeled, seeded and chopped

1/2 cup finely chopped sweet yellow onion

1/2 cup finely chopped green bell pepper

2 jalapeno peppers, seeded and finely chopped

1 Tablespoon sugar

1/2 teaspoon salt

1/2 teaspoon coriander seed, crushed

1 teaspoon finely chopped fresh cilantro

1 1/2 teaspoons finely chopped,
fresh oregano or **1/2 teaspoon** dried

2 Tablespoons corn oil

1 Tablespoon fresh lime juice

1 Tablespoon red wine vinegar

3/4 cup plain tomato sauce

Combine all ingredients; mix well.

Cover and chill 1 hour to allow flavors to blend. Serve with tortilla chips or as a topping for omelets, grilled poultry, meats and fish.

Serves 4+

Cook's notes from Bev and John
Never peeled and seeded tomatoes?
See "Tips and Techniques" chapter for some
hints on making the process quicker and easier.

21

Mango Salsa and Wonton Chips

Ingredients:

1 red bell pepper, halved

1 Tablespoon corn oil

1 cup chopped sweet yellow onion

1 clove garlic, pressed

1/4 cup fresh lime juice

3 Tablespoons finely chopped cilantro

1 jalapeno pepper, seeded and finely chopped

1/4 teaspoon salt

3 medium mangoes

24 wonton wrappers

coarse sea salt

Heat broiler. Place pepper on broiler pan. Broil 3 to 4 inches from heat for 12 to 15 minutes or until skin is blackened. Place pepper in a plastic (careful: plastic will melt if pepper is too hot) or paper bag; close and let cool for 30 minutes. Remove pepper and discard the charred skin (using a knife to help scrape off any stubborn pieces). Finely chop the pepper; set aside.

Heat oil in a 10 inch skillet. Cook onion and garlic over medium heat until tender. Remove from heat; transfer onion mixture to a bowl. Add finely chopped roasted peppers, lime juice, cilantro, jalapeno and salt.

Peel, seed and chop mangoes (should have about 2 cups). Add to the pepper mixture; toss to mix well.

Heat oven to 400F. Lightly spray one side of 24 wonton wrappers with nonstick cooking spray, then sprinkle lightly with sea salt. Cut each wrapper in half diagonally.

Line one or more baking sheets with parchment paper. Arrange wonton triangles, sprayed side up, in a single layer on baking sheets. Bake for 5 minutes or until golden brown and crisp.

Serve Mango Salsa and Wonton Chips.

Serves 6+

Cook's notes from Bev and John
Once you start roasting bell peppers, you'll wonder why you ever ate them any other way!

Corn and Black Bean *Salsa*

Ingredients:

2 1/2 cups frozen kernels of corn, thawed, or fresh, scraped from the cob

16 ounce can black beans, rinsed and drained

1/2 cup finely chopped red bell pepper

1/4 cup finely chopped sweet yellow onion

1 teaspoon finely chopped jalapeno pepper

1/4 cup chopped cilantro

1/3 cup red wine vinegar

1 Tablespoon corn or canola oil

1/4 teaspoon salt

1/4 teaspoon ground black pepper

In a bowl, combine corn, beans, pepper, onion, jalapeno and cilantro.

Stir in vinegar, oil, salt and black pepper until well blended. Cover and refrigerate 1 hour to allow flavors to blend.

Serves 4 to 6

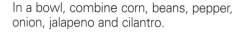

Cook's notes from Bev and John
Great with chips; can also be used as an aside with fish, grilled turkey or chicken.
(Your imagination is your limit to salsa uses.)

"Party Hats" with Smoked Salmon & Edible Confetti

This festive, elegant hors d'oeuvre can easily be prepared a day in advance and assembled just before serving.

Ingredients:

4+ whole wheat croissants, thinly sliced and lightly toasted
8+ thin slices naturally smoked salmon
fresh sprigs of dill

Caper Cream Cheese:

4 ounces softened cream cheese
2 Tablespoons milk
3 Tablespoons capers, drained and patted dry
1 Tablespoon finely minced fresh chives
1/2 teaspoon freshly ground white pepper

Party Pickled Red Onions:

1/2 cup champagne vinegar
2 Tablespoons sugar
1/4 teaspoon freshly ground white pepper
2 Tablespoons finely chopped fresh dill
1 small red onion, sliced into thin rings then coarsely chopped

pizzazz

Edible Confetti:

Coarsely chopped fresh radishes, red bell pepper, yellow bell pepper or other edible "confetti" produce of your choice.

For the Party Pickled Red Onions: Whisk together the vinegar, sugar, pepper and dill in a bowl. Add the onions, tossing to mix well. Set aside at room temperature for up to 4 hours or cover and refrigerate for up to 1 week.

For the Caper Cream Cheese: Combine the cream cheese and milk until creamy; stir in the capers, chives and pepper. Cover and refrigerate (for up to 1 week) until ready to use.

Cut the toasted croissant slices with a 2 inch round cookie cutter. (Store in an airtight container for up to 2 days.)

To assemble: Arrange the salmon slices on a work surface. (Each piece should resemble a rectangle made up of one long straight side, one long irregular side and two shorter sides.) Arrange each slice of salmon so that one of the short sides is facing you.

Spread 1- 2 teaspoons of the cream cheese mixture on the short end and top with a few Party Pickled Red Onions. Roll each piece up from the short end, pinching the long, irregular side tighter, forming a cone shape. (May be covered and refrigerated up to overnight.)

To serve, stand each cone, pointed end up, on a toasted croissant round. Arrange two "Party Hats" on a plate. Sprinkle with the Edible Confetti and stick a sprig of fresh dill into the top of each "hat" to create a feathery flourish. Enjoy!

Scallion Dill Dip

Ingredients:

1/2 cup sour cream, regular, nonfat or less fat

1/4 cup yogurt cheese

1/4 cup chopped scallions

2 teaspoons dried dill weed

1/4 teaspoon salt

1/2 teaspoon freshly ground white pepper

Combine sour cream, yogurt cheese, scallions, dill weed, salt and white pepper in a bowl; mix well.

Cover and refrigerate at least 2 hours to blend flavors. Stir before serving.

Serve with assorted fresh vegetables and crackers, or as an accompaniment to fish.

Makes about 1 cup

Yogurt Cheese

Yogurt cheese is a rich, creamy spread that is an ideal substitute for cream cheese and sour cream. If using in a dessert, treat yourself to vanilla or coffee yogurt cheese by using vanilla or coffee yogurt as the cheese base.

Ingredients:

8 ounces plain yogurt, nonfat

Spoon yogurt into a strainer lined with a coffee filter or several layers of cheesecloth. Place strainer over bowl; cover with plastic wrap.

Refrigerate and let drain overnight. Discard liquid and use cheese left in strainer.

Cover and store up to 5 days in the refrigerator.

Makes about 1/2 cup

pizzazz

Cook's notes from Bev and John
Don't be fooled by recipes that call for draining
the yogurt just a few hours; overnight is best
for extracting as much of the liquid out
of the yogurt and therefore makes the best cheese.

Quick & Easy (Dinner In less than 10 Seconds – Just Kidding!)

- Sautéed Shrimp in Herb Butter

- Apricot Curry Glazed Shrimp

- Southwest Turkey Stew

- Pecan Cheese Balls

- Ravioli with a Fresh Vegetable Sauce

- Hearty Turkey Chili with Corn Dumpling Topping

- Chicken Breasts in Champagne Sauce

- Pollo Con Lima

- Chinese Pork Salad

easy

If you are ever at a loss to support a flagging conversation, introduce the subject of eating.
— *Leigh Hunt*

A recipe is only a theme,
Which an intelligent cook can play each time
with a variation.
— *Madame Benoit*

Appetite is the best sauce.
— *French proverb*

Notes from Bev

Quick has not only to do with prep time but being prepared (just like that Scout motto!). Have a well-stocked assortment of ingredients in the cupboard, freezer and/or fridge. Often, we make a quick stop on the way home to pick up one or two key ingredients, usually perishables, but it's even better if we can head straight home and begin the easy part – cooking.

Easy means, to us, not necessarily few steps but a shorter start to finish. After a hard day, it's the Ravioli with a Fresh Vegetable Sauce or the Shrimp Sautéed in Herb Butter that our mouths are watering for!

These recipes are easy to put together but, as always, remember that the quality of the ingredients has a great deal to do with the finished dish. (You knew we'd get a lecture in there somewhere!) Technique and good equipment can make it easier to cook and, where important to a given recipe, we have noted this. Extra techniques, tips, tidbits and other tantalizing info are also covered in our "Tips and Techniques" chapter.

Sautéed Shrimp in Herb Butter

This is an excellent quick dinner served on a bed of rice or your favorite pasta.

Ingredients:

1 pound uncooked, shell on shrimp

1/4 cup unsalted butter

2 Tablespoons fresh lemon juice

1 Tablespoon fresh parsley, finely chopped

1 teaspoon fresh chives, finely chopped

1/2 teaspoon dried tarragon leaves, crumbled

1/2 teaspoon dried mustard

3/4 teaspoon season salt

1/8 teaspoon cayenne pepper

1 clove garlic, pressed, or **1/8 teaspoon** garlic powder

Shell and devein the shrimp. Melt butter in a large skillet; add lemon juice and seasonings.

Sauté shrimp in hot herb butter over medium heat until pink, turning once. Serve hot.

Serves 4

Cook's notes from Bev and John
For perfectly tender shrimp, cook just until done
(no longer clear in the center).

Apricot Curry Glazed Shrimp

Make yourself a side of couscous with dried, chopped apricots and almonds. Heavenly!

Ingredients:

3 Tablespoons extra virgin olive oil

3 Tablespoons apricot preserves

1 1/2 Tablespoons white wine vinegar

1 Tablespoon Dijon mustard

1 Tablespoon curry powder

2 cloves garlic, pressed

1 1/2 pounds uncooked,
large shrimp, shelled and deveined

shredded lettuce

lemon wedges, optional

fresh apricot halves, optional

Combine oil, preserves, vinegar, mustard, curry powder and garlic in a large bowl.
Add shrimp and toss to coat well. Cover and refrigerate at least 2 hours up to 12 hours.

Heat broiler. Broil shrimp about 6 inches from heat just until cooked through,
about 2 minutes per side.

Place shredded lettuce on plates. Arrange shrimp on top and garnish with lemon wedges
or fresh apricot halves.

Serves 4 to 6

Cook's notes from Bev and John
Too tired after a busy day to let this marinate?
Make it in the morning, cover and refrigerate then
use it that evening for your quickest meal ever!
Remember – overcooked shrimp is tough and rubbery!
After the first 2 minutes of broiling, turn shrimp and estimate
how much cooking time remains to cook completely through.

Southwest Turkey Stew

Delicious served with cornbread.

Ingredients:

1 Tablespoon extra virgin olive oil

1 pound turkey tenderloins, cut into strips

1 cup chopped onions

1 teaspoon dried oregano

1 teaspoon cumin

1 cup picante sauce (mild or hot)

14 1/2 ounce can diced, peeled tomatoes, undrained

1/4 cup cornmeal

1/8 cup unbleached, all purpose flour

1/2 teaspoon ground black pepper

1/2 red bell pepper, cut into chunks

1/2 green bell pepper, cut into chunks

Heat oil in a 12 inch skillet until hot. Add turkey, onions and 2 Tablespoons water; cook and stir until turkey is no longer pink.

Stir in oregano, cumin, 1 cup water, picante sauce and tomatoes. Bring to a boil. Reduce heat; cover and simmer 15 minutes or until turkey is tender.

In a small bowl combine cornmeal, flour and black pepper. Mix well. Slowly stir into stew.

Stir in bell peppers. Cook, uncovered, until bell peppers are crisp tender.

Serves 4

easy

Pecan Cheese Balls

Meat lovers beware - these could turn you into a vegetarian! Basmati rice is a delicious accompaniment.

Ingredients:

2 cups plain, salted crackers, crumbled

1 cup shredded sharp cheddar cheese

1 cup finely chopped pecans

1/2 cup finely chopped onion

6 large eggs

4 cloves garlic, pressed, divided

1 Tablespoon toasted wheat germ

1 teaspoon dried sage

2 Tablespoons corn or canola oil

15 ounce can tomato sauce

6 ounce can tomato paste

1/2 cup chopped red bell pepper

1 Tablespoon dried oregano

1 Tablespoon dried basil

Heat oven to 350F.

In a bowl, mix crumbs, cheese, pecans, onion, eggs, half of the garlic, wheat germ and sage. Shape into 1 to 1 1/2 inch balls.

Heat oil in a large nonstick skillet. Cook pecan cheese balls over medium heat until lightly golden.

Remove with a slotted spoon and place in a single layer in a baking dish.

Meanwhile, make tomato sauce in a bowl by combining can of tomato sauce, tomato paste, bell pepper, remaining garlic, 1 1/4 cups water, oregano and basil. Mix well.

Top pecan balls with tomato sauce mixture. Cover with foil. Bake at 350F for 1 hour until sauce is thick and bubbly.

Serves 4 to 6

Ravioli with a Fresh Vegetable Sauce

Serve with a platter of fresh tomato and mozzarella slices.

Ingredients:

3/4 pound refrigerated cheese ravioli

2 Tablespoons unsalted butter

3 ounces fresh whole green beans
or **1 cup** frozen cut green beans, thawed

1/2 cup thinly sliced carrots

4 ounces sliced fresh mushrooms

1 cup milk, whole or 2%

1 Tablespoon unbleached, all purpose flour

1 Tablespoon chopped fresh basil leaves

1/2 teaspoon salt

1/2 teaspoon freshly ground black pepper

1/4 cup sour cream, regular or lowfat

Cook ravioli to desired doneness. Drain, then rinse with hot water. Keep warm.

Melt butter in a large skillet over medium heat. Add greens beans and carrots; cook until crisp tender (pierce with a fork to test). Add mushrooms, cooking until tender.

In a small bowl, combine milk, flour, basil, salt and pepper; blend well. Add to vegetables in skillet. Cook until mixture thickens and boils, stirring constantly.

Stir in sour cream. Heat thoroughly. Serve vegetable sauce over ravioli.

Serves 3 to 4

Cook's notes from Bev and John

Lowfat and nonfat sour creams have different tastes, and certain brands can be unpleasantly chalky while others are wonderful to use. Find a brand you like and stick with it for cooking.

Hearty Turkey *Chili* with Corn Dumpling Topping

Bev's Hungarian heritage makes her love dumplings and you will, too after tasting this!

Ingredients:

2 Tablespoons canola or corn oil

1 pound lean ground turkey

1 medium onion, chopped

2 16 ounce cans regular stewed tomatoes

2 15 ounce cans light red kidney beans, drained and well rinsed (to remove saltiness)

15 ounce can chickpeas, drained and well rinsed

2 cups tomato sauce (homemade or canned)

2 1/2 cups fresh or thawed, frozen corn kernels

2 teaspoons chili powder

1 1/2 teaspoons ground black pepper

1 cup unbleached, all purpose flour

1/2 cup cornmeal

2 teaspoons baking powder

3/4 cup milk, whole, 2% or skim

Heat oil in a 5 to 7 quart saucepan. Add ground turkey and onion, cooking until turkey is browned, stirring occasionally.

Add stewed tomatoes, kidney beans, chickpeas, tomato sauce, 1 1/2 cups corn, chili powder and black pepper; mix well.

Simmer mixture, uncovered, for 25 minutes to blend flavors, stirring occasionally.

In bowl, combine flour, cornmeal and baking powder. In another bowl, combine milk and remaining 1 cup of the corn. Add milk/corn mixture to dry ingredients, stirring just until dry ingredients are moistened.

Drop dough (rounded Tablespoon size) onto hot chili.

Cover and simmer 20 minutes or until dumplings are fluffy and no longer doughy on bottom (lift dumpling carefully with a large spoon to check for doneness).

Serves 4 to 6

Cook's notes from Bev and John

One of the handiest gadgets for scooping/dropping dough,
shaping cookies and making meatballs is a disher ...
similar to an ice cream scoop but designed
just to – well – dish things out in uniform portions.
Buy quality – a sturdy one will hold up longer
and will be less tiring for your hand/wrist to use.

Chicken Breasts in *Champagne* Sauce

This recipe takes chicken breasts to a new, sophisticated level!

Ingredients:

4 split chicken breasts, skinned and boned

3 Tablespoons unsalted butter

1 teaspoon salt

1/4 teaspoon ground white pepper

1/2 teaspoon dried thyme

1/2 cup chicken broth

1 1/2 cups dry champagne, divided

2 Tablespoons unbleached, all purpose flour

2 egg yolks

Melt butter in a 12 inch skillet. Brown chicken breasts in butter until golden, turning often. Remove chicken to platter.

Add salt, pepper, thyme, broth and 1 1/4 cups of the champagne to pan drippings in skillet. Bring to a boil.

Add chicken, lower heat and cover and simmer for 20 minutes or until chicken is cooked through but still tender. Remove chicken to platter and cover loosely with foil to keep warm.

In bowl, stir flour into remaining 1/4 cup champagne. Stir mixture into liquid in skillet. Cook, stirring constantly, until mixture is thickened and bubbly.

Beat egg yolks in a small bowl. Add about 1/2 cup of the hot sauce to bowl. Stir mixture back into skillet. Heat thoroughly but do not boil.

To serve, spoon a little sauce over each piece of chicken.

Serves 4

Pollo Con Lima

Serve with a Pine Nut Pilaf and Spinach and Strawberry Salad.

Ingredients:

4 split chicken breasts, skinned and boned

1/3 cup extra virgin olive oil

juice of **4** large limes

zest of **1** lime, finely chopped

4 cloves garlic, pressed

4 Tablespoons chopped fresh cilantro

1/2 teaspoon freshly ground black pepper

Lightly pound each chicken breast between waxed
pepper to uniformly flatten them for more even cooking.

Combine oil, lime juice and zest, garlic, cilantro and pepper
in a bowl. Pour over chicken and marinate, covered, for 1 hour.

Grill or broil chicken until just done and juices run clear,
about 2 to 3 minutes per side.

Serves 3 to 4

easy

Cook's notes from Bev and John
This chicken dish is so tasty and so tender that
it's against the law in some States to overcook it –
the chicken becomes dry and tough when overcooked.

Chinese Pork Salad

Delicious simplicity!

Dressing:

1/4 cup rice wine vinegar or sake

2 Tablespoons soy sauce

2 teaspoons sugar

2 teaspoons Chinese chili sauce

1 clove garlic, pressed

Salad:

4 cups shredded Chinese cabbage

1 red bell pepper, halved and cut into thin strips

1/2 cup salted peanuts

2 Tablespoons peanut oil

1 pound pork tenderloin, cut into 1/8 inch slices

In a bowl, combine vinegar, soy sauce, sugar, chili sauce and garlic; blend well.

In large bowl, combine cabbage, red pepper and peanuts.

In skillet, heat oil over medium-high heat. Add pork; stir fry until no longer pink. Drain. Add dressing and warm pork to cabbage mixture; toss gently to coat.

Serves 2+

Pasta! *Pasta!*

- Citrus Herb Pasta Sauce

- Shrimp and Tomato Vodka Sauce

- Tortellini Cashew Salad

- Smoked Salmon and Tortellini Pasta Salad

- Mediterranean Style Penne

- Vegetable Lasagna

- Tomato Macaroni Bake

- Seafood Pasta

- Pasta with Fruits, Nuts and Cheese

- Zucchini, Leek and Poultry Lasagna

- Colorful "Three Bells" Pasta Sauce

- Wonton Chicken Ravioli

- Herbed Tomato Sauce

- Jambalaya Pasta

- Cajun Creole Sauce

- Beurre Noisette Asparagus

41

pasta

Words to Eat By

The honest flavor of fresh garlic is
something I can never have enough of.
— *James Beard, American cooking expert*

… the only classical and true
way to eat pasta is with gusto.
— *James Beard*

Life is a combination of magic and pasta.
— *Federico Fellini, Italian filmmaker*

Food is an important part of a
balanced diet.
— *Fran Lebowitz, American writer*

For a plate of spaghetti, he'd leave home.
For another woman? Never!
— *Adua Pavarotti,
(ex-wife!) of Luciano Pavarotti*

Notes from Bev

John is apt to tell you Bev enjoys anything if it has pasta in it … not quite true, but close!

How could you not enjoy something that comes in such an array of shapes, sizes and flavors? And, if you make your own pasta, shapes are entirely up to your imagination.

A few words before you cook, toss and dig in ….

Forget the oil and salt in the cooking water (oil makes the sauce run off; salt should be added as a sauce ingredient, not cooked into the pasta).

Cook pasta in a large pot of boiling water, stirring gently and often.

Don't boil it until mushy; boil it, as the Italians say, until al dente (tender but firm). Drain and rinse – with hot water if you're serving the pasta hot, with cold water if you're serving the pasta cold – then drain again.

Ingredients to go along with your pasta?
Treat yourself to:

Lots of freshly pressed garlic (invest in a good quality garlic press). Lots of Parmesan cheese (freshly grated only! Yes, buy a wedge of Parmigiano Reggiano and a cheese grater and grate it yourself … you will notice that the freshly grated cheese actually has FLAVOR!).

Don't use a fresh tomato that doesn't look and smell like a tomato (you know what we mean – those hard-as-a-rock, pinkish, picked-before-the-turn-of-the-century tomatoes you see certain times of the year) … if the tomatoes don't look and smell great, move on to another recipe.

Now you're ready to cook, toss, serve and savor!

Citrus Herb Pasta Sauce

Ingredients:

1/3 cup basil infused olive oil

3 cups sliced zucchini (about 1/4 inch thick)

1 cup chopped red onion

1/4 cup grated Parmesan cheese

1/4 cup chopped fresh basil

1/4 cup chopped fresh chives

1/4 cup chopped fresh parsley

2 medium tomatoes cut into wedges

1/2 teaspoon salt

1/2 teaspoon freshly ground black pepper

2 Tablespoons lemon juice

zest of **1** lemon

8 ounces fusilli or rotelle, cooked

Heat oil in a 12 inch skillet; add zucchini and onion.

Cook over medium heat, stirring occasionally, until zucchini are crisp tender.
Add basil, chives, parsley, tomatoes, Parmesan, salt, pepper, lemon juice and zest.

Cover and remove from heat; let stand until tomatoes are heated through, about
3 minutes. Serve with fusilli or rotelle pasta.

Serves 4+

Shrimp and Tomato *Vodka* Sauce

Easy and elegant - with that extra something that vodka adds to this simple sauce!

Ingredients:

1 Tablespoon unsalted butter

28 ounce can (Italian) plum tomatoes

1/4 cup chopped fresh basil

salt and freshly ground black pepper, to taste

1/2 cup vodka

6 Tablespoons heavy cream

1 pound uncooked, large shrimp, shelled and deveined

1 pound mostaccioli, rigatoni or ziti pasta, cooked

Crush plum tomatoes with their liquid in a large bowl using a spoon, fork or potato masher. Set aside.

Melt butter in a 12 inch skillet over medium heat. Add tomatoes with their juices and bring to a boil.

Reduce heat, add chopped basil and simmer 15 minutes. Season to taste with salt and freshly ground black pepper.

Add vodka and heavy cream and boil for 2 to 3 minutes. Add shrimp, reduce heat and simmer just until the shrimp are cooked through, turning occasionally.

Serve sauce with freshly cooked pasta.

Serves 4

Tortellini Cashew Salad

This salad is extravagantly rich! Enjoy...!

Ingredients:

8 ounces sun-dried tomatoes, packed in oil

1/3 cup extra virgin olive oil

1 Tablespoon fresh lemon juice

2 cloves garlic, pressed

1 teaspoon freshly ground black pepper

1/4 teaspoon salt

8 ounces marinated artichoke hearts, drained and quartered

1 pound tortellini, egg or spinach, cooked

1/4 pound cashew halves

Drain tomatoes, reserving 1 Tablespoon of the oil. Coarsely chop tomatoes; set aside.

Combine reserved oil, olive oil, lemon juice, garlic, pepper and salt in a large serving bowl.
Stir in tomatoes and artichoke hearts. Add tortellini. Stir gently to combine.

Cover and refrigerate one hour to allow flavors to blend. Just before serving, toss with cashews.

Serves 6+

pasta

Cook's notes from Bev and John

Instead of discarding remaining oil from drained sun-dried tomatoes, refrigerate in a covered container and use in salad dressings and marinades.

45

Smoked Salmon and Tortellini Pasta Salad

Ingredients:

1/4 cup sour cream

1/4 cup plus **1 Tablespoon** extra virgin olive oil

3 Tablespoons fresh lemon juice

2 Tablespoons Dijon mustard

1 Tablespoon dry white wine

1/4 teaspoon ground white pepper

3/4 pound fresh cheese tortellini,
cooked

1/2 cup thinly sliced red onion

1/4 cup chopped fresh chives

1/4 cup chopped fresh dill

2 Tablespoons capers, drained

4 ounces smoked salmon,
cut into thin strips

In a small bowl, whisk together sour cream,
1/4 cup olive oil, lemon juice, mustard, wine and
white pepper. Cover and chill dressing until ready to use.

Transfer tortellini to serving bowl. Add remaining
1 Tablespoon olive oil to tortellini; toss to coat.

Add red onion, chives, dill and capers, stirring gently to blend.

Add salmon and enough dressing to coat and toss well.

Serves 4 to 6

Mediterranean Style Penne

Ingredients:

8 bacon slices, chopped

1 cup chopped onion

1 small eggplant, cut into 1 inch cubes

2 cups chopped, peeled and seeded tomatoes

4 cloves garlic, pressed

1 Tablespoon red wine vinegar

1 teaspoon dried thyme

1/3 cup capers, rinsed and drained

salt and freshly ground black pepper, to taste

1 pound penne pasta, cooked

1 Tablespoon extra virgin olive oil

1 1/2 cups feta cheese, crumbled

1/2 cup pitted Kalamata olives

1/4 cup chopped fresh parsley

Cook bacon in a 10 inch skillet until crisp. Transfer to paper towels using a slotted spoon, reserving drippings in skillet.

Add onion and eggplant to skillet. Sauté in bacon drippings over medium-high heat until eggplant is tender and golden, about 20 minutes. Add tomatoes, garlic, vinegar and thyme. Reduce heat to medium and cook 5 minutes. Stir in capers. Season with salt and pepper.

Transfer pasta to a large serving bowl. Toss with olive oil. Mix in eggplant sauce, feta, olives and bacon. Sprinkle with parsley and serve.

Serves 4 to 6

pasta

Cook's notes from Bev and John
Black, brine-cured Kalamata olives are available at
Greek and Italian markets as well as most supermarkets.
An olive pitter works best for the task of pitting, but
a paring knife and a careful hand will do the job.

Vegetable Lasagna

Ingredients:

2 teaspoons corn or canola oil

3 cups unpeeled, diced eggplant*

3/4 cup chopped onion

1 clove garlic, pressed

28 ounce can crushed tomatoes

1 1/4 teaspoons salt, divided

1/2 teaspoon sugar

1/2 teaspoon dried basil

1 pound carrots, peeled and shredded

12 ounces fresh spinach, cleaned, stemmed and chopped

2 cups ricotta cheese

1 cup shredded mozzarella cheese

1 large egg, beaten

1/4 teaspoon nutmeg

9 lasagna noodles, cooked

1/4 cup grated Parmesan cheese

Heat oil in a 12 inch skillet over medium-high heat. Add eggplant, onions and garlic; cook and stir for 5 minutes. Stir in tomatoes, 1 teaspoon of the salt, sugar and basil. Bring to a boil; reduce heat, cover and simmer until eggplant is tender.

Heat oven to 375F.

Bring 2 quarts water to boil. Add carrots and spinach and cook 1 minute; drain well. Combine carrots, spinach, ricotta, mozzarella, egg, remaining salt and nutmeg in a large bowl. Mix well.

Spoon 1 1/4 cups eggplant/sauce mixture into a 13x9 inch baking pan. Layer with three lasagna noodles and half the spinach mixture, three more noodles and 1 1/4 cups sauce, then remaining spinach and noodles. Top with any remaining sauce.

Sprinkle with Parmesan cheese. Bake, uncovered, 30 to 40 minutes until hot.

Serves 8

Cook's notes from Bev and John
*John would want you to peel the eggplant; your choice!

Tomato Macaroni Bake

Crusty bread and a greens salad complete this hearty dish.

Ingredients:

1 pound large elbow macaroni, cooked

1 cup extra virgin olive oil

9 cloves garlic, pressed

1 cup chopped onion

1 Tablespoon sugar

1 teaspoon dried red pepper flakes

1/2 cup chopped fresh basil

1/4 cup chopped fresh oregano

3 cans (1 pound 12 ounces each) tomatoes

1/4 cup grated Parmesan cheese

Place the pasta in a large bowl. Pour all of the olive oil over, toss well, and let sit for 1 hour.

Pour pasta into a strainer set over a deep saucepan, letting excess oil drain into saucepan.

Add garlic, onion, sugar, pepper, basil and oregano to saucepan. Heat over medium heat until the oil gets very hot, about 10 minutes. Remove from the heat and cool to room temperature.

In a large bowl, crush the tomatoes with a spoon, fork or a potato masher and add with their juices to the saucepan.

Heat the oven to 400F. Place the macaroni in a large roasting pan; pour mixture in saucepan over macaroni and stir well.

Bake, uncovered, for 40 minutes, carefully mixing with a heatproof spatula every 10 minutes to ensure that all the pasta cooks evenly. Serve with Parmesan cheese.

Serves 4+

Seafood Pasta

Treat yourself to this extravagant dish!

Ingredients:

1 cup heavy cream

1 cup whole milk

3 Tablespoons vodka

zest of **1** lemon

4 ounces cream cheese,
room temperature, cut into small bits

4 ounces smoked salmon, cut into thin strips

4 Tablespoons unsalted butter

1/2 cup finely chopped red onion

3 plum tomatoes (medium size), seeded
and chopped

3 Tablespoons chopped fresh dill

1 Tablespoon chopped fresh tarragon

1 pound scallops (cut into pieces, if using
sea scallops)

1/4 teaspoon salt

1 1/2 teaspoons freshly ground black pepper

1 pound capellini or vermicelli, cooked

Combine the cream, milk, vodka and lemon zest in a 4 to 5 quart saucepan. Heat to boiling
and continue to cook until reduced by half.

Remove saucepan from heat; stir in the cream cheese and smoked salmon. Set saucepan aside.

Melt the butter in a 9 inch skillet over medium high heat. Add the onion and tomatoes and cook,
stirring occasionally, for 10 minutes. Add the dill and tarragon and cook for 2 minutes longer.

Add the tomato mixture, scallops, salt and pepper to the cream mixture. Heat over medium heat
until the sauce is hot and the scallops are just cooked through.

Toss the sauce with the cooked pasta. Serve at once.

Serves 4+

Pasta with Fruits, Nuts and Cheese

Sweet, salty, fruity and crunchy ... this dish offers an incredible array of tastes.

Ingredients:

3 ripe pears, Bartlett or D'Anjou

3/4 cup unsalted butter

1/2 cup pecans, lightly toasted and coarsely chopped

1 1/2 cups Gorgonzola cheese, crumbled

1 cup grated Asiago or Parmesan cheese

1 pound fettuccine or linguine, cooked

Core pears and cut into 1/4 inch to 1/2 inch thick wedges.

In a 12 inch skillet or sauté pan, melt butter over medium heat, stirring occasionally, until light golden in color. Sauté pears in butter over medium heat, turning often, until softened.

Add pecans and Gorgonzola, stirring until Gorgonzola is melted. Stir in 3/4 cup Asiago or Parmesan. Remove pan from heat.

Gently toss together freshly cooked pasta and pear mixture until well combined. Sprinkle with remaining Asiago or Parmesan cheese.

Serves 4+

Cook's notes from Bev and John

Toast pecans in a dry skillet over low heat until fragrant, watching carefully so they don't burn.

Zucchini, Leek and Poultry *Lasagna*

An overnight sensation . . . do ahead, using uncooked lasagna noodles!

Ingredients:

1 1/2 Tablespoon unsalted butter, divided

3 cups skinned, boned chicken or turkey pieces, uncooked

4 cloves garlic, pressed, divided

1 pound fresh mushrooms, sliced

5 cups thinly sliced leeks

3 Tablespoons unbleached, all purpose flour

2 1/2 cups milk, whole or 2%

1 1/2 cups grated Parmesan cheese

1 cup ricotta cheese

1/2 teaspoon dried basil

1/4 teaspoon freshly ground black pepper

1/4 teaspoon salt

12 lasagna noodles, uncooked

5 cups coarsely shredded zucchini

Melt 1/2 Tablespoon of the butter in a 12 inch skillet over medium heat.
Add chicken or turkey and 2 cloves of the garlic; sauté until poultry is done.
Remove from skillet; set aside.

Add remaining garlic and mushrooms to skillet; sauté until liquid evaporates. Set aside.

Melt remaining 1 Tablespoon butter in a 6-quart saucepan over medium heat; add leeks.
Cover and cook 30 minutes, stirring occasionally. Sprinkle with flour, stirring until well blended.

Gradually add milk, stirring occasionally. Cook over medium heat until thickened, stirring constantly. Add poultry, 1/2 cup Parmesan cheese, ricotta, basil, pepper and salt. Blend well.

Arrange 4 lasagna noodles in the bottom of a greased 13 x 9 x 2 inch baking pan. Top with half of the zucchini, 1/3 cup Parmesan cheese, half the mushroom mixture and 2 cups poultry mixture.

Repeat layers, ending with lasagna noodles. Spread the remaining 2 cups poultry mixture over noodles; sprinkle with remaining 1/3 cup Parmesan cheese. Cover and chill 8 to 12 hours.

Heat oven to 350F. Bake, covered, for 1 hour. Uncover and bake an additional 15 minutes.

Let stand 10 minutes before serving.

Serves 4+

Cook's notes from Bev and John

Use only uncooked noodles; overnight, the uncooked noodles absorb liquid from the vegetables. The noodles will soften while baking and produce a creamy lasagna.

Colorful "Three Bells" Pasta Sauce

Ingredients:

2 Tablespoons extra virgin olive oil

2 medium red bell peppers cut into strips

2 medium orange bell peppers cut into strips

2 medium yellow bell peppers cut into strips

2 cloves garlic, pressed

2 medium tomatoes cut into wedges

1 Tablespoon chopped fresh oregano
or **1 teaspoon** dried

1 Tablespoon chopped fresh basil
or **1 teaspoon** dried

1/2 teaspoon salt

1/2 teaspoon freshly ground black pepper

3/4 cup grated Parmesan cheese

8 ounces bow tie or penne pasta, cooked

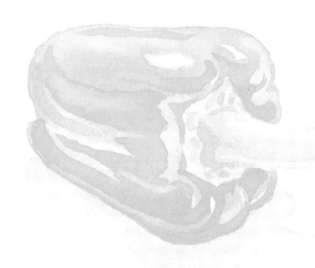

Heat olive oil in a 12 inch sauté pan. Lightly sauté peppers and garlic for 2 minutes.

Add tomatoes, cooking until peppers are crisp tender. Add oregano, basil, salt and pepper; blend well.

Place pasta in a large serving bowl; top with pepper sauce and toss gently to blend. Sprinkle with Parmesan cheese and serve immediately.

Serves 4 to 6

Wonton Chicken Ravioli

Ingredients:

6 ounces ground, raw chicken
1 cup soft cream cheese with chives and onion
1/4 cup shredded carrot
1 jalapeno pepper, seeded and finely chopped
20 3 1/2 inch wonton wrappers
Herbed Tomato Sauce (see next recipe)

Bring water to a boil in a 6 to 8 quart stockpot.

In a bowl, stir together chicken, cream cheese, carrot and jalapeno. Set aside.

Place about 1 teaspoon filling in the center of each wrapper. Brush edges with water. Fold one corner over to the opposite corner, forming a triangle.

To seal, press edges together with fingers or tines of a fork.

Drop ravioli into boiling water. Reduce heat and simmer, uncovered, for 4 minutes or until chicken is no longer pink. (To check for doneness, quickly and carefully remove one ravioli and cut open to test.)

Remove ravioli with a slotted spoon. Drain.

Ladle warm Herbed Tomato Sauce over ravioli and serve.

Serves 4+

Cook's notes from Bev and John
Uncooked ravioli may be frozen for up to 3 months.
To cook frozen ravioli, drop into boiling water directly
from freezer, cooking for 6 to 7 minutes.

Herbed Tomato Sauce

Sugar helps "mellow out" the acidity in tomatoes.

Ingredients:

2 cups chopped onions

2 cloves garlic, pressed

1/3 cup extra virgin olive oil

12 to 14 medium size, coarsely chopped, peeled and seeded tomatoes

1 Tablespoon dried oregano
or **3 Tablespoons** finely chopped, fresh

1 teaspoon sugar

1 teaspoon dried basil leaves
or **1 Tablespoon** finely chopped, fresh

1 teaspoon dried rosemary leaves, crushed,
or **1 Tablespoon** finely chopped, fresh

1/4 teaspoon salt

1/4 teaspoon freshly ground black pepper

12 ounce can tomato paste

In a 6-quart stockpot cook onions and garlic in oil until tender.

Add tomatoes, oregano, sugar, basil, rosemary, salt, pepper, 2 cups water and tomato paste; bring to a boil, stirring occasionally.

Reduce heat; simmer, uncovered, for 1 hour stirring occasionally.

If not using immediately, store in the refrigerator for up to 1 week or in the freezer for up to 3 months.

Yield: about 8 to 10 cups

Cook's notes from Bev and John

Keep a supply of this sauce in 1- or 2-cup containers in your freezer. When used in place of canned tomato sauce, it's a delicious way of helping reduce sodium in your diet.

Jambalaya Pasta

This is an adaptation of a meal we had in New Orleans.
The combination of cheeses makes this dish that much more outstanding!

Ingredients:

1 cup cubed skinless, boneless chicken breast

1 cup sliced chorizo sausage

3 Tablespoons chopped ham or
uncooked shrimp, shelled and deveined

1 Tablespoon peanut oil

1/2 cup red bell pepper, cut into strips

1/4 cup red onion, cut into strips

2 cloves garlic, pressed

1 Tablespoon unsalted butter

1 1/2 cups Cajun Creole Sauce

1/3 cup shredded Provolone cheese

1/3 cup shredded smoked Gouda cheese

3/4 pound rotini or fusilli pasta, cooked

Heat oil in a 12 inch skillet until hot. Cook chicken, sausage and ham or shrimp until chicken is no longer pink; remove meats from skillet, draining off any excess fat. Set aside and keep warm.

Return skillet to heat and add pepper, onion, garlic and butter. Cook until onion is tender. Add meats to skillet, then add the Cajun Creole Sauce; boil.

Place pasta in a large serving bowl and top with sauce. Sprinkle with cheeses, tossing gently to mix.

Serves 4 to 6

pasta

Cajun Creole Sauce

Delicious tossed with hot cooked pasta, or use in our Jambalaya Pasta recipe!

Ingredients:

3 Tablespoons extra virgin olive oil

1/2 cup chopped green bell pepper

1/4 cup chopped onion

1/4 cup chopped celery

2 Tablespoons sliced scallions

2 cloves garlic, pressed

1 Tablespoon finely chopped fresh Italian parsley

1/2 teaspoon sea salt

1/2 teaspoon sugar

1/2 teaspoon dried basil

1/4 teaspoon cayenne pepper

1/2 teaspoon freshly ground black pepper

1/2 teaspoon freshly ground white pepper

2 bay leaves

Heat oil in a 4-quart saucepan. Add bell pepper, onion, celery, scallions, garlic, parsley, salt, sugar and basil. Stir to blend.

Add cayenne pepper and black and white peppers; add bay leaves.

Cook until vegetables are crisp tender, stirring occasionally. (This will take about 10 minutes.) Remove bay leaves.

Use immediately or refrigerate, covered, until ready to use.

Beurre Noisette Asparagus

The rich, distinctive taste of this simple dish is excellent with fish.

Ingredients:

8 ounces medium-to-wide egg noodles, cooked

2 1/2 cups 1 inch pieces of fresh asparagus

1/2 cup unsalted butter

1 teaspoon freshly ground black pepper

Cook asparagus in a 10 inch skillet in a small amount of boiling water just until crisp tender; drain. Add noodles to skillet, keep warm.

Make beurre noisette (browned butter): Cook butter in a 2-quart saucepan until butter turns light golden brown, stirring constantly. Immediately pour butter over noodles and asparagus; add pepper. Toss to coat and serve.

Serves 4+

pasta

Cook's notes from Bev and John
If you're tempted to use margarine in place
of the butter in this recipe, move on!

Seafood: Beyond Fishsticks

- Pignoli Salmon

- Double Salmon Cakes with John's Homemade Tartar Sauce

- Salmon Oven Poached in Ohio Cider

- Swordfish with Blood Orange and Onion Relish

- Creole Style Tilapia

- Devilish Haddock

- Mustard Meringue Sole

- Sole "Lasagna"

- Lemon Marinated Albacore Tuna

- Pepper Tomato Orzo Fish

- Creole Style Scallops, Shrimp and Fish

- Fish Ranchero

- Macadamia Crusted Sea Bass with Thai Red Curry Sauce

Words to Eat By

Recently I sat across from a person who was deliberately eating clams; She'd open up a shell, and there, in plain view, would be this stark naked clam, brazenly showing its organs ... if a restaurant is going to serve these things there should be little loincloths on them.
— *Dave Berry, American humorist*

Fish to taste right, must swim three times – in water, in butter and in wine in the stomach.
— *James de Coquet, French food writer*

The kitchen is a country in which there are always discoveries to be made.
— *Grimod de la Reyniere*

Food is meant to tempt as well as nourish, and everything that lives in water is seductive.
— *Jean Paul Aron*

Fish and visitors stink in three days.
— *Benjamin Franklin*

Notes from Bev

One of our favorite foods – so flexible, so quick and easy to prepare.

The biggest fear people have is how to cook seafood and tell when it's done, and the most common mistake in preparing seafood is overcooking it!

If you cook shrimp and scallops until they just lose their translucence (until white all the way through) they will be perfect – tender and tasty. If you go beyond, they become tough and stringy and lose flavor. Cut into a shrimp and scallop to check; it's the most accurate test.

Fish should be cooked just until it begins to flake. A fork twisted in the flesh will start to flake when done. Some fish flake more easily than others; e.g. trout will flake quickly and dramatically at the done point while tuna and other firm-fleshed fish will not flake as easily when tested. Again, cutting into the steak or fillet is the ultimate test of doneness to see the change of color – from translucent to milky white in the case of a white fish or raw (moist) and dark-looking to a drier look in the case of tuna or salmon.

Students will ask us how to keep the house from smelling like fish! Remember, when you cook chicken or beef the house smells like chicken or beef and you don't complain! Anyway –

Truly fresh fish should smell like the ocean or fresh water when purchased. If it smells "off" (strong fishy and old or ammonia like) don't buy it. Use fresh seafood within 24 hours. If you buy a beautiful piece of fish and your plans change, freeze it immediately (we usually wrap in plastic wrap then foil) for use within a month.

When you get your fresh seafood home, place it in a stainless, glass or porcelain dish and cover with plastic wrap placed against the seafood, keeping out as much air as possible. Top the plastic wrap with fresh lemon slices and your refrigerator will remain odor free (at least from seafood!).

As an aside, a seafood monger you can trust is a great asset in ordering ahead or getting help with substitutions ... and worth the price for freshness and quality. Seek out an independent seafood market or get to know the seafood manager at the best specialty market near you.

Don't be afraid to cook seafood – try these tremendous recipes, using our cooking tips, and you will prepare seafood dishes better than most dishes you've had when you've eaten out!

So: get the rest of the meal ready, prepare one of our seafood selections, and enjoy immediately when done!

Pignoli Salmon

An adaptation of an outstanding recipe served at Café Panache in Bev's home state of New Jersey.

Ingredients:

1/2 cup soft bread crumbs (white tastes best)

4 salmon steaks (6 ounces)

2 Tablespoons Dijon mustard

3/4 cup chopped pine nuts

1 teaspoon lemon infused olive oil

1/4 cup and **1 Tablespoon** unsalted butter

2 Tablespoons fresh lemon juice

1/4 cup heavy cream

1/4 teaspoon salt

1/4 teaspoon freshly ground white pepper

Heat oven to 350F. Brush the Dijon mustard evenly on one side of the salmon steaks.

Combine crumbs and pine nuts. Pat evenly on top of the mustard.

Heat oil with 1 Tablespoon of the butter in a 12 inch ovenproof skillet over medium heat until oil/butter mixture foams. Cook salmon, crumbs side down, until golden brown.

Carefully turn fish over. Transfer skillet to oven and bake 7 to 10 minutes more until salmon is cooked through.

Meanwhile, cook lemon juice in a 1-quart saucepan until reduced to 1 teaspoon. Add cream and boil until slightly thickened. Whisk in butter, a piece at a time, until smooth.

Add salt and pepper. Serve sauce with salmon.

Serves 4

Double *Salmon* Cakes

Ingredients:

8 Tablespoons peanut oil, divided

1/3 cup finely chopped onion

1/2 cup finely chopped red bell pepper

2 1/2 cups soft bread crumbs (white bread tastes best), divided

1/2 cup finely chopped fresh parsley

1 pound uncooked salmon fillets or steaks, coarsely chopped

4 ounces smoked salmon, coarsely chopped

1 large egg

1 large egg yolk

1 teaspoon Dijon mustard

1 teaspoon Worcestershire sauce

1 teaspoon hot pepper sauce

1/4 teaspoon cayenne pepper

Heat 4 Tablespoons of the peanut oil in a 12 inch skillet.
Add onion and bell pepper and cook until softened. Transfer to a large bowl.

Mix in 1 1/4 cups of the bread crumbs and the parsley. Toss in both types of the salmon; add egg, yolk, mustard, Worcestershire, hot pepper sauce and cayenne pepper. Cover and refrigerate until well chilled (up to 4 hours).

Divide mixture into ten cakes, flattening each into a circle. Coat cakes in remaining breadcrumbs. Heat 2 Tablespoons of the peanut oil in the cleaned 12 inch skillet over medium heat. Cook a few fish cakes at a time in a skillet until golden brown on both sides and cooked through, flattening them slightly with a spatula. Serve cakes with John's Homemade Tartar Sauce.

Serves 2 to 4

with John's Homemade *Tartar* Sauce

Sauce:

3/4 cup mayonnaise

1 1/2 Tablespoons sweet pickle relish

1 Tablespoon chopped fresh tarragon

1 teaspoon lemon juice

zest of **1** lemon, finely chopped

1/4 teaspoon hot pepper sauce

Mix all ingredients in a small bowl. Cover and refrigerate at least 1 hour to allow flavors to blend. (May be prepared up to 2 days ahead.)

Makes 1 cup

seafood

Salmon Oven Poached in Ohio Cider

Ingredients:

2 cups fresh Ohio apple cider

1 medium onion, thinly sliced

1 1/2 teaspoons salt

1/2 teaspoon freshly ground black pepper

1/2 teaspoon cinnamon

1 whole salmon, cleaned and scaled
and about **6 pounds**

Heat oven to 375F. In a 2-quart saucepan, combine 2 cups water, cider, onion, salt, pepper and cinnamon. Heat to boiling over high heat.

Place fish in a deep baking pan. Pour cider mixture over fish. Cover tightly with lid or foil.

Bake salmon until fish flakes easily when tested with a fork at its thickest part – begin checking after 35 minutes.

Remove from poaching liquid and serve immediately. Salmon can also be refrigerated in cooking liquid and served cold as an appetizer.

Serves 4+

Cook's notes from Bev and John
Okay, you could use fresh cider from your home state!

Swordfish with Blood Orange and Onion Relish

Ingredients:

1 pound swordfish steaks, 3/4 inch thick

1/2 cup freshly squeezed orange juice

2 Tablespoons brown sugar

2 Tablespoons red wine vinegar

2 medium blood oranges, peeled, seeded and chopped

1/2 cup finely chopped red onion

2 Tablespoons chopped fresh parsley

1 jalapeno pepper, seeded and finely chopped

1 clove garlic, pressed

Combine juice, brown sugar and vinegar in a 10 inch skillet. Bring mixture to a boil. Reduce heat and simmer, uncovered, until mixture becomes syrupy; stirring often. Remove from heat.

Place swordfish on a greased rack of a broiler pan. Brush both sides of swordfish with 1 Tablespoon of the juice mixture.

Broil 4 inches from heat for 6 to 8 minutes or until fish begins to flake.

For relish, combine the blood oranges, onion, parsley, jalapeno and garlic in a bowl. Add remaining juice mixture, tossing gently to mix.

Serve fish with relish.

Serves 2 to 4

Cook's notes from Bev and John
For some additional heat and a burst of color,
substitute habanero for the jalapeno pepper.

Creole Style *Tilapia*

Ingredients:

2 Tablespoons peanut oil

3/4 cup chopped onion

1/2 cup chopped celery

1/2 cup chopped red bell pepper

1 clove garlic, pressed

16 ounce can diced tomatoes in juice

2 Tablespoons chopped fresh parsley

1 bay leaf

1 teaspoon hot pepper sauce
(or more to taste)

1/2 teaspoon dried thyme

1 pound tilapia fillets

hot cooked rice

Heat the oil in a 12 inch nonstick skillet over medium-high heat until hot.

Add the onions, celery, pepper and garlic and cook until the vegetables are crisp tender.

Add the tomatoes, wine, parsley, bay leaf and hot pepper sauce. Bring the mixture to a boil. Reduce the heat; cover and simmer, stirring occasionally, for 30 minutes.

Add the thyme, then place the fillets on top of the tomato mixture. Cover and cook until the fish flakes easily with a fork. Remove bay leaf and discard.

Remove the fillets to a serving plate and top with some of the sauce. Serve with hot cooked rice and the remaining sauce.

Serves 2 to 4

Cook's notes from Bev and John
Catfish may be substituted for the tilapia in this recipe.

Devilish *Haddock*

Ingredients:

1 pound haddock steaks

2 Tablespoons unsalted butter, melted

3/4 cup shredded Cheddar cheese

1/4 cup chili sauce

1 teaspoon Dijon mustard

1/2 teaspoon prepared horseradish

1/2 teaspoon hickory flavored sauce (liquid smoke)

Heat broiler. Place haddock on a well-greased rack of a broiler pan.

Brush fillets with melted butter. Broil 4 inches from the heat until fish
just begins to flake when tested with a fork, about 8 minutes. Do not turn.

Blend cheeses, chili sauce, mustard, horseradish and hickory sauce.
Spread over fillets.

Broil to melt the cheese, watching carefully not to burn, about 3 minutes longer.

Serves 2 to 4

Cook's notes from Bev and John
Fresh halibut is another great fish for this recipe.

Mustard Meringue *Sole*

This recipe is a definite WOW!

Ingredients:

2 sole fillets

1/2 teaspoon salt

1/4 teaspoon freshly ground white pepper

1 Tablespoon unsalted butter, melted

2 large egg whites

1/4 cup freshly grated Parmesan cheese

2 Tablespoons Dijon mustard

1 Tablespoon finely chopped onion

zest of **1** lemon, finely chopped

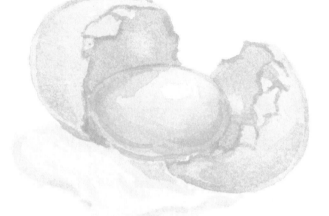

Heat broiler. Sprinkle fillets lightly with salt and pepper.
Place fish on a greased rack of a broiler pan; brush with
1 Tablespoon of the melted butter.

Broil fish with tops 3 inches from heat until light brown, about 3+ minutes (depending
on thickness of the fillets). Do not turn.

Whip egg whites until stiff but not dry. Fold in cheese, mustard, onion and lemon zest.
Spread egg mixture with a wooden spoon or heat-resistant spatula over fish.

Broil until tops are golden brown. Watch carefully – this takes one minute or so.

Serves 2+

Cook's notes from Bev and John
Put everything else on hold when you make
this recipe – your cell phone, your pager –
give people a chance to miss you and enjoy!

Sole "Lasagna"

Ingredients:

1/2 cup unsalted butter

1 clove garlic, pressed

1 1/2 teaspoons dried basil

1 teaspoon finely chopped onion

1/2 teaspoon salt

4 sole fillets, cut into 8 equal-size pieces

1 large tomato, cut into 4 slices

4 slices mozzarella cheese

3 Tablespoons freshly grated Romano cheese

Heat oven to 350F. Melt butter in oven in a 13x9 inch baking dish.

Add garlic, basil leaves, onion and salt to butter; stir to blend. Dip both sides of sole into melted butter.

Set four sole fillet pieces aside. Place remaining four pieces in same baking dish; layer each with one tomato slice and one slice of mozzarella.

Top each cheese slice with remaining sole pieces. Sprinkle fillets with Romano cheese.

Bake near center of 375F oven for 25 minutes or until fish flakes with a fork. To serve, spoon the remaining butter from bottom of the baking dish over fillets.

Serves 2 to 4

seafood

Lemon Marinated Albacore *Tuna*

Ingredients:

4 albacore tuna steaks,
about **6 ounces** each and 1 inch thick

4 Tablespoons extra virgin olive oil

1/4 teaspoon salt and freshly ground black pepper

4 teaspoons mustard seed

1 Tablespoon chopped fresh oregano
or **1 teaspoon** dried

3 Tablespoons fresh lemon juice

1/4 teaspoon red pepper flakes

2 cloves garlic, pressed

In a shallow baking dish blend the oil, black pepper, mustard seed, oregano, lemon juice,
red pepper flakes and garlic. Add the tuna and coat on both sides.

Cover dish with plastic wrap and let stand at room temperature for 30 minutes or refrigerate
up to 2 hours.

Heat a 12 inch nonstick skillet. Place the tuna in the very hot skillet. Cook for 3 minutes;
turn the tuna, brushing with remaining marinade, and continue cooking for another 3 to 4 minutes.

Serve medium rare (tuna is DRY when cooked to well done!).

Serves 4

Pepper Tomato Orzo *Fish*

Ingredients:

6 ounces orzo, cooked, drained, rinsed and kept warm

1 Tablespoon olive oil

1/2 cup chopped onion

1 clove garlic, pressed

28 ounce can plum tomatoes, drained and cut up

1/4 cup dry white wine

2 Tablespoons tomato paste

1 teaspoon dried oregano

1/4 teaspoon salt

1/2 teaspoon freshly ground black pepper

1 pound cod fillets, cut into 4 pieces

1/3 cup crumbled feta cheese

Heat olive oil in a 10 or 12 inch skillet. Cook onion and garlic over medium heat until onion is tender.

Add tomatoes, wine, tomato paste, oregano, salt and pepper. Bring to a boil, mixing well.

Add fish; reduce heat, cover and simmer 8 to 10 minutes or until fish flakes easily.

With a slotted spatula, place fish on cooked orzo. Add feta cheese to tomato mixture, mixing well. Spoon mixture over orzo and fish fillets to serve.

Serves 2 to 4

seafood

Creole Style Scallops, Shrimp and Fish

Ingredients:

1 Tablespoon peanut oil

1/4 cup finely chopped scallions

1 clove garlic, pressed

16 ounce can tomato pieces in juice

1/3 cup tomato paste

1 1/2 cups chopped red bell pepper

1 jalapeno pepper, seeded and finely chopped

1 teaspoon sugar

1/4 teaspoon thyme leaves

1/2 teaspoon cayenne pepper, divided

1 teaspoon hot pepper sauce

1/3 pound shrimp, shelled and deveined

1/3 pound scallops

2 Tablespoons unsalted butter

1 1/2 pounds fish fillets

1/4 teaspoon salt

2 Tablespoons lemon juice

In a 12 inch skillet, sauté scallions and garlic in oil until tender.
Stir in tomatoes, tomato paste, red bell pepper, jalapeno, sugar, thyme,
and 1/4 teaspoon of the cayenne pepper and the hot pepper sauce.

Simmer mixture 20 minutes, stirring occasionally. Stir in shrimp and scallops;
simmer just until shrimp and scallops are done.

Heat oven to 450F. Melt butter in a 13x9 inch pan. Place fish in melted butter, turning to coat.
Sprinkle lightly with salt, remaining cayenne pepper and lemon juice. Bake at 450F for
7 to 10 minutes or until fish is done. Serve shrimp/scallop mixture over cooked fish.

Cook's notes from Bev and John
Any white fleshed, mild flavored fish such
as tilapia, haddock, sole, cod, orange roughy
or halibut can be used for this recipe

Fish Ranchero

Inspired by a delightful fish dish we had in a southwest restaurant.

Ingredients:

4 tilapia fillets
1 1/2 cups finely crushed tortilla chips
3/4 teaspoon chili powder
5 Tablespoons lime juice
2 Tablespoons peanut oil
1 1/2 cups salsa
chopped fresh cilantro

Heat oven to 450F. Line a baking sheet with parchment paper.

Cut each fillet in half lengthwise and pat dry with paper towels.

Mix crushed tortilla chips and chili powder in a shallow dish. In another shallow dish, mix lime juice and oil.

Dip tilapia in the lime mixture, and then immediately dredge in the seasoned tortilla crumbs to coat. Place on prepared baking sheet.

Sprinkle fish with any remaining crumbs. Bake 8 to 10 minutes or until crisp and golden and fish flakes easily when tested with a fork.

Warm salsa in a small saucepan over low heat. Arrange tilapia on serving plates and spoon salsa across the center. Sprinkle with fresh cilantro and serve.

Makes 4 servings

seafood

Macadamia Crusted Sea Bass

This is an adaptation of an outstanding recipe we had during our travels in Chicago. Feel free to use any sweet white fish as a substitute for the sea bass in this recipe.

Ingredients:

1 cup toasted macadamia nuts

2 cups unbleached, all purpose flour

2 large eggs, beaten to blend

sea salt and freshly ground white pepper

4 6 ounce sea bass fillet pieces (about 1 inch thick)

1/4 cup extra virgin olive oil

Thai Red Curry Sauce

chopped fresh basil

chopped toasted macadamia nuts

Heat oven to 450F. Finely chop nuts with 1 cup flour in the processor. Transfer mixture to pie plate. Place remaining 1 cup flour in another pie plate. Place beaten egg in another pie plate.

Lightly coat fish with plain flour, shaking off excess. Dip fish into egg, then into nut mixture being sure to coat well.

Heat oil in a large ovenproof skillet. Add fish and cook until golden brown and crusty, about 5 minutes. Turn fish and transfer the skillet to the oven and roast for about 4 minutes or until fish is just cooked through. (This may take longer depending on the thickness of the fish.)

To serve: heat Thai Red Curry Sauce and ladle onto plates. Place fish in center. Garnish with chopped basil and nuts.

Makes 4 servings

with Thai Red *Curry* Sauce

This is a spectacular sauce - use it on grilled chicken or atop cellophane noodles for a dynamite side dish. It freezes well, too.

Ingredients:

1 Tablespoon extra virgin olive oil

1 1/2 cups chopped onion

1 1/2 Tablespoons Thai Red Curry Paste or Thai Roasted Red Chile Paste

3 cups chicken broth

1/2 cup unsweetened coconut milk

1/4 cup lime juice

2 Tablespoons fish sauce (nam pla)

1 clove garlic, pressed

1 Tablespoon arrowroot or cornstarch

Heat oil in a medium saucepan over low heat. Add onion; sauté until translucent. Add curry paste, stirring to blend.

Add broth and coconut milk. Boil for 10 minutes. Stir in lime juice, fish sauce and garlic. Simmer until mixture is reduced by half.

Mix 2 Tablespoons water with the arrowroot/cornstarch in a small bowl until smooth. Whisk into sauce. Simmer until thick, whisking often.

Cool. Purée in saucepan with immersion blender or in batches in a blender.

seafood

Cook's notes from Bev and John

Although we dearly love sea bass, as of this writing it's an endangered fish. Let's replenish it and use another whitefish instead!

Soups : Hot & Cold

Words to Eat By

Good manners: the noise you don't make when you're eating soup.
— *Bennett Cerf*

It's probably illegal to make soups, stews and casseroles without plenty of onions.
— *Maggie Waldron*

Salt is the policeman of taste: it keeps the various flavors of a dish in order and restrains the stronger from tyrannizing over the weaker.
— *Malcolm de Chazal*

Only the pure of heart can make a good soup.
— *Ludwig van Beethoven*

I would often ask the butcher for a few bones "for my dog" ... then I would make the most exquisite soup of those bones .... It was several years before my butcher realized that I didn't have a dog.
— *Edward Giobbi*

Cold soup is a very tricky thing and it is the rare hostess who can carry it off. More often than not the dinner guest is left with the impression that had he only come a little earlier he could have gotten it while it was still hot.
— *Fran Lebowitz*

Worries go down better with soup.
— *Yiddish proverb*

To make a good soup, the pot must only simmer or "smile."
— *French proverb*

Notes from Bev

I must confess – I love fresh bread and homemade soup.

One of my fondest Sunday memories as a child was stopping on the way home from church ....

First stop: an Italian bakery to buy (still warm) Vienna bread (the entire loaf never made it home); Second stop: the Hungarian restaurant in New Brunswick where they would fill our soup pot with lovingly made chicken soup with fine, homemade noodles ....

Home meal replacement at its finest!

The many times my Mom made homemade soups I always begged for her dumplings, too – those doughy creations that floated atop our individual bowls of beef or chicken soup when they weren't smothered with paprikash! As I got older, I was always experimenting with my own dumpling creations – some lemon zest here, some grated carrots and fresh herbs there – endless possibilities!

And, as an adult, I've grown to love the refreshing burst of flavors from cold fruit soups – especially as an appetizer or dessert!

Block out some time for yourself and make one of our soup creations; then relax and savor the flavors. Create some new memories for your family or just yourself.

80

Beef Soup and Carrot Basil *Dumplings*

Ingredients:

1 pound beef sirloin or tenderloin, cubed

2 small onions, quartered

1 Tablespoon unsalted butter

6 cups beef broth

1 1/4 teaspoons salt, divided

1/2 teaspoon freshly ground black pepper

1 bay leaf

2 cups sugar snap peas, trimmed

3 medium carrots, diagonally sliced into 1/2 inch pieces

2 stalks celery, diagonally sliced into 1/2 inch pieces

2 teaspoons sweet Hungarian paprika

3/4 cup unbleached, all purpose flour

1/4 cup finely shredded carrots

1 teaspoon baking powder

1/4 teaspoon salt

1 teaspoon finely chopped fresh basil

1/4 cup milk, 2% or whole

1 Tablespoon canola or corn oil

1 large egg, lightly beaten

Brown beef and onions in butter in an 8-quart stockpot. Add broth, 1 teaspoon of the salt, pepper and bay leaf. Bring to a boil. Reduce heat; cover and simmer 1 to 1 1/2 hours or until beef is tender.

Add sugar snap peas, sliced carrots, celery and paprika. Simmer, covered, until vegetables are crisp tender. Remove bay leaf.

Prepare dumplings: combine flour, shredded carrots, baking powder, remaining 1/4 teaspoon of the salt and basil; blend well. Add milk, oil and egg; stir into dry ingredients just until moistened.

Bring soup to a boil. Drop dumpling dough by rounded Tablespoons onto boiling soup. Reduce heat to simmer; cover tightly and cook about 8 minutes or until dumplings are fluffy and no longer doughy on bottom.

Serves 4

Baked *Brie* Soup

Simply elegant! We've given a sophisticated twist to a panade!

Ingredients:

1 Tablespoon unsalted butter

1 cup diced mushrooms

1 cup finely chopped shallots

1 clove garlic, pressed

4 cups chicken broth

1/2 cup half-and-half or heavy cream

1/4 teaspoon salt

1/2 teaspoon freshly ground white pepper

8 ounces Brie (rind removed) cut into 8 pieces

8 1/3 inch thick French baguette slices, toasted

Melt butter in a 3-quart saucepan over medium heat.

Add mushrooms, shallots and garlic and cook until shallots are softened.

Add broth and boil until reduced by a third. Strain into another saucepan.

Add half-and-half to strained mixture and boil until slightly thickened.
Season soup with salt and white pepper.

Heat oven to 400F. Place one piece of Brie in each of four ovenproof soup bowls.
Ladle soup into each. Place two pieces of baguette in each. Top with remaining Brie.

Bake until bubbling.

Serves 4

Chicken Panade

An adaptation of a classic French recipe enjoyed by us at several fine restaurants.

Ingredients:

1/4 cup unsalted butter

3 cups coarsely shredded cabbage

1 cup thinly sliced carrots

1 cup chopped onions

3 split chicken breasts, skinned and boned and cut into thin strips

12 slices French baguette, at least 1/2 inch thick, toasted

4 Tablespoons grated Parmesan cheese

3 3/4 cups chicken broth

1 1/3 cups shredded Swiss cheese

Heat oven to 350F.

Melt butter in a 12 inch skillet. Add cabbage, carrots, onions and chicken. Cook until chicken is cooked and vegetables are tender, stirring occasionally.

Place four slices of the bread in bottom of an ungreased 3-quart casserole. Spoon half of the cabbage mixture over bread; sprinkle with one-third of the Parmesan cheese.

Repeat with four more slices of bread, remaining cabbage mixture and then half the remaining Parmesan cheese.

Top with remaining bread. Pour chicken broth over all. Bake, uncovered, at 375F for 25 minutes.

Remove from oven and sprinkle with the Swiss cheese and remaining Parmesan cheese. Bake an additional 25 minutes or until edges are bubbly.

Serves 2 to 4

Cook's notes from Bev and John
Toast bread slices in a 325F oven just until crisp.

Minestrone Soup Mix with Cabernet

A wonderful gift for yourself or friends.

Ingredients:

1/4 cup dried split peas

1/2 cup dried kidney beans

4 teaspoons beef bouillon granules

1 teaspoon dried basil

1 teaspoon dried oregano

1 teaspoon dried parsley

1 teaspoon salt

1 teaspoon freshly ground black pepper

1 cup small elbow macaroni

Combine the peas, beans, beef bouillon, basil, oregano, parsley, salt and pepper in a bowl. Stir to blend and store in an airtight container. Store the macaroni separately in an airtight container.

To make the minestrone soup with cabernet from the mix:

1 container Minestrone Soup Mix with elbow macaroni

1 pound mild or hot Italian sausage, skinned and sliced

2 carrots, peeled and sliced

2 ribs celery, sliced

1/2 cup chopped onion

28 ounce can diced tomatoes

1 1/2 cups Cabernet

Combine 8 cups water with the Minestrone Soup Mix (set macaroni aside for now) in an 8 quart stockpot and simmer for 1 1/2 hours.

In a 10 inch skillet brown the sausage. Add the vegetables to the skillet and sauté for 5 minutes.

Add the sausage, vegetables and tomatoes to the soup. Bring the soup to a boil and add the elbow macaroni. Simmer for 10 minutes.

Slowly stir in the Cabernet and continue to simmer for 20 minutes or until macaroni is tender.

Serves 4 to 6

Cellophane Noodle *Spinach* Soup

A light, delicate soup, perfect as a first course with a stir-fry dinner.

Ingredients:

2 ounces cellophane noodles

6 cups chicken broth

1 Tablespoon dry white wine

2 teaspoons freshly grated ginger

1/4 teaspoon salt

2 cloves garlic, pressed

1/4 teaspoon soy sauce

1 pound baby spinach, cleaned, stems removed

1 teaspoon sesame oil

In a small bowl, soak the noodles in warm water to cover until pliable, 20 to 30 minutes. Drain and rinse, then cut with kitchen shears into 4 inch lengths.

In a 4-quart saucepan, combine the chicken broth, wine, ginger, salt, garlic and soy sauce. Cover and bring to a boil over high heat.

Stir in spinach just until the leaves are wilted.

Stir in the noodles and bring back to a boil. Remove from the heat and stir in the sesame oil.

Serves 2 to 4

soups

Pasta and Bean Soup

Ingredients:

1 cup sliced onion

2 cloves garlic, pressed

1 cup chopped, smoked ham

2 Tablespoons olive oil

16 ounce can diced tomatoes in juice

1 teaspoon dried oregano

1/2 teaspoon dried thyme

1/2 teaspoon freshly ground black pepper

1 cup elbow macaroni

2 medium red skin potatoes, cut into 1/2 inch pieces

15 ounce can garbanzo beans, rinsed and drained

1 small zucchini, thinly sliced

1/3 cup freshly grated Romano cheese

Cook onion, garlic and ham in oil in a 5-quart stockpot over medium heat until onion is tender. Add tomatoes, 3 cups water, oregano, thyme and pepper. Heat to boiling.

Stir in macaroni and potatoes; reduce heat. Cook, uncovered, until macaroni is tender, about 10 minutes. Stir in beans and zucchini. Cook just until zucchini is crisp tender. Serve, sprinkling each serving with Romano cheese.

Serves 2 to 4

Toasted Tortilla and Bean Soup

Ingredients:

6 small flour tortillas, each cut into 10 wedges

1 Tablespoon vegetable oil

1 1/2 cups coarsely chopped onions

2 cloves garlic, pressed

16 ounce can diced tomatoes in juice

2 cups diced zucchini

15 ounce can garbanzo beans,
rinsed and drained

15 ounce can black beans,
rinsed and drained

4 ounce can chopped green chilies

2 teaspoons chili powder

1 teaspoon whole cumin seed, crushed

1/2 teaspoon dried oregano leaves

1/2 teaspoon salt

1/4 teaspoon cayenne pepper

In a 12 inch skillet, put tortilla wedges in a single layer. Cook over medium heat until lightly browned and crisp. Cook in batches, if necessary. Remove from skillet.

Heat oil in a 5-quart saucepan; add onion and garlic and cook, stirring, until onion is tender.

Add tomatoes, zucchini, beans, chilies, chili powder, cumin seed, oregano, salt and cayenne pepper; add 2 cups water. Cover and bring to a boil, then reduce heat and simmer 30 minutes or until zucchini is tender.

Serve soup in wide individual bowls topped with toasted tortilla wedges.

Serves 2 to 4

Chilled *Raspberry* Soup

A wonderful appetizer, dessert or palate cleanser between courses.

Ingredients:

2 10 ounce packages frozen red raspberries,
unsweetened preferred, thawed

1 cup cran-raspberry juice

3/4 cup superfine sugar

3 whole cloves

1 cinnamon stick

1 Tablespoon lemon juice

8 ounces low fat raspberry yogurt

1 pint fresh red raspberries

In a blender container, place thawed frozen raspberries and 1/4 cup of water; blend until smooth.

In a 5-quart stockpot combine puréed fruit, 1 1/4 cups water, cran-raspberry juice, sugar, cloves and cinnamon stick. Cook over medium heat until mixture begins to boil; remove from heat and cool completely.

Strain mixture into a large bowl. Add lemon juice and raspberry yogurt, whisking until well blended.

Cover; refrigerate until thoroughly chilled. Pour into individual serving dishes.
Top with fresh red raspberries.

Serves 2+

Chilled *Strawberry* Soup

Ingredients:

1 quart fresh strawberries, washed and hulled
plus **10** additional strawberries

1 cup freshly squeezed orange juice

1 1/4 teaspoons instant (quick) tapioca

1/8 teaspoon freshly grated nutmeg

1/2 teaspoon ground cinnamon

1/2 cup superfine sugar

zest from **1** orange, finely chopped

1 Tablespoon lemon juice

1 cup low fat buttermilk

Purée 1 quart of the strawberries in a food processor; strain into a 4-quart saucepan.
Add orange juice, blending well.

In a small bowl, mix tapioca with 4 Tablespoons of the puréed strawberry mixture.
Let stand 10 minutes. Add to saucepan with nutmeg and cinnamon.

Heat, stirring constantly, until mixture comes to a boil. Cook 1 minute or until thickened.
Remove from heat.

Pour soup into a large bowl. Add sugar, orange zest, lemon juice and buttermilk. Blend well.

Slice remaining 10 strawberries and fold into soup. Cover soup and refrigerate at least 4 hours.

Serves 4

Cook's notes from Bev and John

This is spectacular served in a hollowed out decorative
melon bowl for a soup tureen, topped with thin slices
of blood oranges.

Thrilling *Grilling*

grilling

The story of barbecue is the story of America;
Settlers arrive on a great unspoiled continent,
discover wondrous riches, set them on fire
and eat them.
— *Vince Staten*

Everything tastes better outdoors.
— *Claudia Roden*

Most people hate the taste of beer – to begin
with. It is, however, a prejudice that many
people have been able to overcome.
— *Winston Churchill*

Notes from Bev

A few words about equipment: a table along
side your grill is a plus. Space is often needed for
baste, tools, a towel, long mitts, a timer, recipes,
a cutting board, a knife, spices, a serving platter
and your favorite beverage (a requirement for
socializing and story telling!).

We frequently use a good porcelain covered
steel grid (in place of skewers) for delicate fish
and smaller pieces of meat or vegetables.
Smoking wood chips are another favorite of ours,
and we have mentioned fruit wood, mesquite,
hickory or grape in several recipes.

Grilling is one of our favorite methods of cooking
(well, John's favorite because Bev does the
clean up!), and the following recipes are sure
to become your favorites, too. Enjoy their
varied tastes.

When Henry Ford invented charcoal briquets (a way to use up scrap wood leftover from Model T production), he probably didn't realize what he was starting!

Today there is every type of grill imaginable, even "professional" models with an assortment of fancy extras, and almost everyone has access to some type of grilling apparatus.

If you are a charcoal griller, it is best to start your coals with an electric starter or charcoal chimney. (We don't recommend fluids or fluid-soaked briquets since they can impart an objectionable flavor to the food being grilled.)

Many of our recipes suggest the Indirect Method of grilling. The purpose of the Indirect Method is to avoid flare ups which blacken the outside of the grilled food and undercook the inside, ruining it! This Indirect Method places the food over a drip pan (usually a disposable rectangular aluminum pan) or in the case of a gas grill to the side which has no flame (i.e. one burner off).

The most important tip to remember when grilling is to be able to tell when your food is done. There are many uncontrollable factors such as weather, temperature, wind, etc., which can change drastically the amount of time required to get that "piece of meat" to just the right degree of doneness.

It seems to me that, when John is teaching, after making this very point he claims to be the better cook. What a sense of humor he has ….

Even though this may sound basic, we like to use a timer so we can check our progress or add another coat of baste.

As far as testing goes, we use an instant read thermometer on thicker pieces of meat or fish, and, always, a cut into the thickest part will show you exactly whether you are done or not. A fork is used to check vegetables to your desired degree of doneness.

Probably the two biggest mistakes most people make when grilling is failure to use the Indirect Method of grilling (when recommended) and overcooking.

A Trio of *Barbecue Sauces*

Please remember: any remaining basting sauce that is to be served along side grilled foods must be properly heated before serving it. Always heat remaining sauce to boiling before serving. Another option (and the one we prefer) is to divide the sauce into two portions one part to be used for basting and the other to be served as a sauce with the grilled foods.

Shaffer's Barbecue Sauce

1 Tablespoon unsalted butter

2 cups finely chopped onions

2 cloves garlic, pressed

1 stalk celery, chopped

1 cup chopped green bell pepper

28 ounce can stewed tomatoes

12 ounce can tomato paste

1 Tablespoon dry mustard

1 Tablespoon salt

1 bay leaf, broken

1/2 cup cider vinegar

1/2 cup molasses

1 Tablespoon hot pepper sauce

1 Tablespoon liquid smoke

juice of **one** lemon

Melt butter in a 5-quart saucepan. Add onion, garlic, celery and pepper. Cook until tender but not brown. Add stewed tomatoes, tomato paste, dry mustard, salt, bay leaf, vinegar, molasses, hot pepper sauce, liquid smoke and lemon juice. Bring to a boil.

Reduce heat and cover. Simmer for one hour, stirring occasionally. Remove from heat. Allow to cool. Remove bay leaf.

Purée in a blender or force through a food mill. Keep refrigerated, covered, for up to 7 days.

Makes about 3 pints. Use on anything you barbecue.

Cook's notes from Bev and John
This sauce freezes very well.

All American Barbecue Sauce

4 Tablespoons unsalted butter

3 cups finely chopped onion

3 cups ketchup

3/4 cup packed light brown sugar

3/4 cup Worcestershire sauce

1/2 cup prepared, bottled steak sauce

1 teaspoon cider vinegar

1/4 teaspoon hot pepper sauce

Heat the butter in a 4-quart saucepan over medium heat. Add the onions and cook until tender but not brown.

Add ketchup, brown sugar, Worcestershire, steak sauce, vinegar, 1 cup water, and hot pepper sauce. Bring to a boil over high heat, then reduce the heat and simmer, stirring occasionally, for 20 minutes.

Store any leftovers covered in the refrigerator for up to 7 days.

Cook's notes from Bev and John
Freeze this one, too!

John's Finest Barbecue Sauce

1/3 cup packed light brown sugar

1 Tablespoon cornstarch

1 teaspoon chili powder

1 cup tomato sauce

1/2 cup ketchup

1/2 cup cider vinegar

1/2 cup dark corn syrup

1/4 cup orange liqueur

In a 4-quart saucepan, stir together the brown sugar, cornstarch and chili powder.
Add the tomato sauce, ketchup, 1/2 cup water, vinegar and corn syrup, stirring to combine.

Bring the mixture to a boil. Reduce heat to low and simmer, uncovered, for 30 minutes, stirring occasionally.

Add the orange liqueur. Return the mixture to boiling, then reduce heat and simmer the sauce, uncovered, for 5 additional minutes. Store, covered, for 7 days in the refrigerator. (Guess what? This sauce freezes well!)

Cook's notes from Bev and John
Delicious basted over your favorite pork or poultry
about the last half of grilling.

Apricot Hens grilling

Ingredients:

1 large can and **1 small can** apricot halves (in light syrup)

3/4 cup apricot preserves

3/4 teaspoon ground ginger

4 fresh or frozen (thawed) Cornish Hens
(about 3/4 to 1 pound size)

salt and ground black pepper

Prepare grill.

Combine apricots, preserves and ginger in a 4-quart saucepan.
Cook over medium heat for 10 minutes, stirring occasionally.
Remove saucepan from heat. Set aside to cool.

With kitchen shears, cut each hen along backbone then along breastbone to cut in half.
Rinse hens and pat dry. Rub each half with salt and ground black pepper.

Brush halves on both sides with apricot mixture. Grill, skin side down (indirect) for
10 to 15 minutes or until golden.

Turn and rebrush, cooking until done. Serve hens with any remaining sauce on the side.

Serves 4 to 6

Cook's notes from Bev and John
Be sure to cook to a boil any remaining sauce
before using to serve on the side.

Mushroom, Mozzarella and Sourdough *Appetizer*

Ingredients:

1/4 cup balsamic vinegar

2 shallots, finely chopped

3 Tablespoons finely chopped, drained, oil-packed, sun-dried tomatoes

1 to 2 Tablespoons finely chopped fresh basil

2 cloves garlic, pressed

1 Tablespoon chopped fresh parsley

1/2 teaspoon finely chopped fresh rosemary

1/2 cup extra virgin olive oil

1/4 teaspoon cayenne pepper

1/8 teaspoon salt

16 fresh shiitake mushrooms, stemmed

10 to 15 pieces mozzarella cheese, about 1 inch cube size

1 loaf sourdough bread, sectioned lengthwise

1 red bell pepper, seeded and cut into chunks

2 yellow squash, cut in half lengthwise then into 1 inch pieces

2 zucchini, cut the same as yellow squash

Combine balsamic vinegar, shallots, sun-dried tomatoes, basil, garlic, parsley and rosemary. Gradually whisk in oil. Whisk in cayenne pepper and salt. Set vinaigrette aside.

Prepare grill (medium heat). Place mushrooms, red bell pepper and squashes in well-oiled grill basket or on a grid. Brush with vinaigrette mixture.

Grill (indirect) until vegetables are lightly browned and tender, basting once or twice with vinaigrette and turning occasionally (about 8 minutes).

With about two minutes left of grill time, brush bread with vinaigrette. Place bread, sliced sides down, over direct heat until browned. Remove bread; cut into veggie-size pieces.

Place mozzarella pieces in large serving bowl. Immediately toss hot veggies with cheese (to allow cheese to soften slightly); add bread pieces. Add some additional vinaigrette and toss well.

Serves 3 to 4

Cook's notes from Bev and John
To make this a meal, toss hot cooked pasta into the bowl with the veggies and cheese. Grill bread and serve as slices on the side.

Wine Country *Beef* Tenderloin

A spectacular way to marinate and grill beef tenderloin!

Ingredients:

3 to 4 pound beef tenderloin, trimmed

1 cup dry red wine, such as Cabernet Sauvignon

1/3 cup extra virgin olive oil

1/2 cup chopped onion

1/3 cup chopped fresh parsley

2 cloves garlic, pressed

1 bay leaf

1/2 teaspoon salt

1 teaspoon freshly ground black pepper

1 cup hickory wood chips, soaked in water for 30 minutes before grilling

Stir together wine, oil, onion, parsley, garlic, bay leaf, salt and pepper. Pour over beef that has been placed in a glass or porcelain baking dish. Cover and refrigerate 4 hours or up to overnight; turn meat several times to distribute marinade during this time.

Prepare grill.

Drain hickory chips and place on coals. Lift beef from marinade and set on grill. Cook (indirect) covered, turning every 10 minutes for even browning, until a meat thermometer inserted in center registers 130F for rare, 155F for medium-rare, about 40 minutes. May be cooked longer according to your doneness preference.

Transfer beef to a platter and let stand 15 minutes before slicing and serving.

Serves 6

grilling

Horseradish Butter Topped Salmon

Grill some bell peppers, zucchini and fresh asparagus to toss with horseradish butter and serve with the salmon!

Ingredients:

1/3 cup unsalted butter, room temperature
2 Tablespoons prepared horseradish
zest of **1** lemon
1/2 teaspoon freshly ground black pepper
1 salmon fillet, about 1 1/2 pounds
1 Tablespoon extra virgin olive oil
1/4 teaspoon salt

Prepare grill.

Stir together butter, horseradish, zest and black pepper in a small bowl. Set aside.

Brush salmon on both sides with oil; place on well-oiled grill grid. Sprinkle salt over salmon.

Grill (indirect) covered, 5 minutes on each side or just until cooked through. Brush immediately with horseradish butter.

Serve salmon with remaining horseradish butter.

Serves 2

Turkey Veggie Burgers

Ingredients:

1 celery stalk

3 scallions

2 cloves garlic, pressed

1 1/4 pounds ground turkey

1/2 pound turkey sausage, casings removed

1/2 cup grated zucchini, squeezed dry

1 Tablespoon finely chopped fresh oregano
or **1 teaspoon** dried

1 1/4 teaspoons ground black pepper

1 Tablespoon clover honey

2 teaspoons soy sauce

3 tomatoes, cut into 1/2 inch thick slices

slices of mozzarella cheese

Prepare grill.

Finely chop celery and scallions. Place in a bowl with the garlic.

Add to bowl turkey, sausage, zucchini, oregano, pepper, honey and soy sauce; mix until combined. Shape into 4 to 6 patties.

Grill (direct), turning after 5 minutes, until just cooked through. Grill tomatoes 5 minutes, turning once, until bubbly.

Immediately top burgers with mozzarella slices, then tomato slices and serve. Serve on your favorite sourdough or multigrain bun.

Serves 4 to 6

Cook's notes from Bev and John
Not all ground turkey is created equal. For best flavor
and less fat, request turkey ground from white meat only
(no skin, please!).

Wine Country Grilled *Shrimp*

Serve over a bed of couscous with wedges of fresh fruit on the side.

Ingredients:

1 1/2 cups dry white wine

1 1/2 cups extra virgin olive oil

3/4 cup chopped fresh basil

2 Tablespoons coarsely ground black pepper

40 large shrimp, peeled and deveined

10 to 12 thin lemon slices

Combine wine, oil, basil and black pepper. Place shrimp in shallow porcelain or glass baking dish. Pour marinade over.

Cover and refrigerate at least 3 hours (or up to 6 hours), turning occasionally.

Prepare grill.

Drain shrimp, reserving marinade. Thread skewer through center of shrimp, interspersing with lemon slices. (Or place shrimp and slices of lemon on a well-oiled grill grid.)

Grill shrimp (indirect) until just opaque, basting occasionally with reserved marinade, about two minutes per side.

Serves 4 to 6

Cook's notes from Bev and John

Remember, overcooked shrimp will be tough and rubbery! And rubbery shrimp is like a rubber chicken – good for a laugh only.

Tuna with Pineapple Salsa

Ingredients:

2 shallots, finely chopped

2 cloves garlic, pressed

1 cup finely chopped red onion

1 cup finely diced red bell pepper

1 jalapeno pepper, seeded and finely chopped

1 pineapple, peeled, cored and cut into 1 inch cubes

1 teaspoon saffron threads

1/2 cup brown sugar

1/4 cup dry sherry

1 cup rice wine vinegar or sake

1 cup coarsely chopped cilantro

1 Tablespoon extra virgin olive oil

2 Tablespoons coarsely ground black pepper

sea salt

6 tuna steaks (about 8 ounces each), 1 inch thick

Combine shallots, garlic, red onion, red bell and jalapeno peppers, pineapple, saffron, brown sugar, sherry and vinegar in a 4-quart saucepan. Simmer over medium-low heat for 20 minutes, stirring frequently.

Mix in the cilantro and set aside.

Prepare grill.

Brush tuna with oil. Rub the pepper onto the tuna steaks and lightly salt.

Grill tuna over high heat (indirect) turning once until medium rare, about 3 minutes per side.

Slice and serve with salsa.

Serves 4 to 6

Cook's notes from Bev and John

Tuna is best served rare to medium rare. Here's what I tell my students: If you like it well done, buy canned; if you've never tried it with some red/pink in the center, close your eyes and eat it and enjoy the fresh, moist taste!

Halibut with Creamy *Guacamole* Sauce

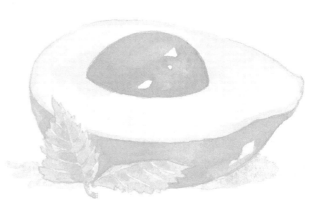

Ingredients:

1 ripe avocado

4 teaspoons fresh lime juice

4 Tablespoons dry white wine

3 Tablespoons finely chopped scallions

1/4 teaspoon ground cumin

1/8 teaspoon cayenne pepper

5 Tablespoons plain, nonfat or lowfat yogurt
(drained of excess water)

4 halibut steaks (1/2 pound each),
cut 3/4 inch to 1 inch thick

olive oil for brushing fish

Prepare grill.

Peel and pit avocado. In food processor, purée the avocado, lime juice, wine,
scallion, cumin, cayenne and yogurt. Scrape down sides and reblend until smooth.
Transfer sauce to a small bowl and set aside.

Brush halibut on both sides with olive oil. Grill (indirect) on a well-oiled grid for 4 to 5 minutes
on each side or until it just flakes. Serve with sauce.

Serves 3 to 4

Peppered Beef Tenderloin

A fantastic combination of tastes and textures - peppery, creamy, tangy, zesty, fruity - WOW!

Ingredients:

1 cup thinly sliced red onion

2 Tablespoons extra virgin olive oil

1/3 cup dry red wine

1/4 cup cranberry juice

4 teaspoons prepared horseradish

1/2 cup sour cream, regular or lowfat

1/2 teaspoon Worcestershire sauce

1 pound beef tenderloin, cut into 1 inch cubes

5 Tablespoons coarsely ground black pepper

Cook onion in oil in a 10 inch skillet over medium heat until very soft and golden brown.

Add wine and juice; boil until three-fourths of the liquid has evaporated. Cool to room temperature. Cover and chill until ready to serve.

In bowl, combine horseradish, sour cream and Worcestershire sauce. Mix well; cover and chill until ready to serve.

Prepare grill.

Roll tenderloin pieces in pepper. Grill (direct) on well-oiled grill grid over medium coals for 12 to 14 minutes or until desired doneness, turning once halfway through cooking.

Serve with some of the horseradish sauce and some of the red onion "marmalade."

Serves 2 to 4

Cook's notes from Bev and John
If using a lowfat sour cream, be sure to taste it
before you cook with it. Some have a chalky aftertaste.

Very Sophisticated *Chops*

These are not your Mother's pork chops (although she'd like them!).

Ingredients:

1/2 cup light brown sugar

1 Tablespoon cornstarch

1 teaspoon chili powder

1 cup tomato sauce

1/2 cup white wine vinegar

1/2 cup ketchup

1/2 cup dark corn syrup

1/4 cup orange liqueur

4 thick, center-cut pork chops, fat removed

In a 4-quart saucepan combine brown sugar, cornstarch and chili powder. Stir in tomato sauce, vinegar, ketchup, corn syrup and 1/2 cup water. Bring mixture to boiling.

Reduce heat. Simmer, uncovered, 30 minutes. Stir in orange liqueur. Simmer, uncovered, for 5 additional minutes.

Prepare grill.

Baste chops and cook (direct) until done, about 4 minutes per side. Brush again with baste when turning.

Reheat remaining sauce to boiling. Serve grilled chops with additional sauce.

Serves 4

Cook's notes from Bev and John
This sauce is also delicious with lamb, beef or poultry!

Grilled *Bananas* Foster

Add a festive New Orleans dessert to your grilling repertoire!

Ingredients:

4 Tablespoons unsalted butter

1/2 cup light brown sugar

2 Tablespoons light rum

4 to 5 large, firm, ripe bananas, peeled and sliced

1/2 gallon vanilla ice cream or frozen yogurt

Prepare grill.

Melt butter on the grill in a large disposable aluminum pan.

Add brown sugar and rum. Cook until mixture boils, stirring occasionally.

Add bananas; stir gently. Cook until bananas are hot, being careful not to overcook so bananas don't get "mushy."

Serve immediately over ice cream.

Serves 4+

grilling

Jamaican Pineapple Wedges

Ingredients:

1 ripe pineapple
3/4 cup light rum
1/4 cup clover honey
2 Tablespoons light brown sugar
1 Tablespoon unsalted butter

Cut off green crown from top of pineapple. Cut pineapple in half lengthwise. Cut each half lengthwise into 3 wedges.

Remove core from each wedge; cut each wedge crosswise into 1 inch slices, cutting to (but not through) the skin. Set aside.

Prepare grill.

Combine rum, honey, brown sugar and butter in a 1-quart saucepan. Bring to a boil. Remove from heat; set aside.

Place pineapple on a well-oiled grill grid and cook 30 minutes (indirect) until lightly browned. Turn and baste with rum mixture every 10 minutes.

Serve warm.

Serves 4+

Cook's notes from Bev and John
Delicious with chicken, pork or as a dessert!

Spectacular *Salads* : A Main Event

- Chinese Chicken Salad

- Jerk Chicken Salad

- Lobster Salad, What's Cooking? Style

- Tarragon Chicken Salad, Too!

- Smoked Turkey Salad

- Smoked Salmon and Tortellini Salad

- A Toss of Steak, Beans and Pasta

- Deli Pasta Salad

- Curried Chicken Salad, What's Cooking? Style

- Chorizo, Artichoke and Three Bean Salad

- Tuscan Bread Salad with Tomatoes,
  Onions and Olives

- "Meatless" Taco Salad

salads

You need to have the soul of a rabbit to eat lettuce as it is usually served – green leaves slightly lubricated with oil and flavored with vinegar. A salad is only a background; it needs embroidering.
— *Paul Reboux*

To make a good salad is to be a brilliant diplomatist – the problem is entirely the same in both cases. To know how much oil must mix with one's vinegar.
— *Oscar Wilde*

This would be a better place for children if parents had to eat spinach.
— *Groucho Marx*

Notes from Bev

Main dish salads are an excellent way to combine taste and healthful ingredients into an easy meal. The combination of flavors from around the world give excitement to these diverse recipes. Call it fusion cooking, ethnic diversity, a melding of tastes, or just a dynamite combination of ingredients – these salads are spectacular!

Entertaining someone special? Wow them with Lobster Salad, What's Cooking? Style, or our Curried Chicken Salad.

Breaking up a relationship? Serve Jerk Chicken Salad!

Pour yourself a glass of wine, serve one of these delicious main dish salads and enjoy!

Chinese Chicken Salad

Serve with a side of chow mein noodles and little else!

Ingredients:

1/2 cup soy sauce

1/4 cup vegetable oil

1/4 cup dry sherry

2 Tablespoons honey

2 teaspoons brown sugar

3 cups diced, cooked chicken

8 ounces linguine

6 ounces snow peas, cooked

1 pound Chinese cabbage, thinly sliced

8 ounce can water chestnuts, drained and sliced

1/2 cup cashews, toasted

2 scallions, thinly sliced

Combine soy sauce, oil, sherry, honey and brown sugar in a bowl; blend well.
Place chicken in another bowl, pouring half of soy mixture over chicken. Mix well.
Cover and refrigerate chicken mixture 2 to 4 hours. Reserve remaining dressing.

Break linguine in half. Cook, drain, rinse and set aside.

Place linguine in serving bowl. Gently stir in snow peas, Chinese cabbage, bell pepper,
water chestnuts, cashews, scallions and remaining dressing.

Add refrigerated chicken mixture. Serve immediately.

Serves 6

Jerk Chicken Salad

This salad is versatile! Besides making a delicious showing as a main event, you could easily turn this into an appetizer using celery pieces or Belgian endive leaves for "holders."

Ingredients:

2 teaspoons sugar

1 teaspoon dried thyme

1 teaspoon ground cinnamon

1/2 teaspoon ground white pepper

1/4 teaspoon salt

1/4 teaspoon cayenne pepper

1/4 teaspoon freshly ground nutmeg

1/8 teaspoon ground cloves

2 split chicken breasts, skinned, boned and cubed

1 Tablespoon peanut oil

1/4 cup finely chopped onion

1 ounce fully cooked ham, chopped

1/2 cup chopped fresh pineapple

1 cup seeded and finely chopped tomato

1/4 cup sour cream

Stir together sugar, thyme, cinnamon, white pepper, salt, cayenne, nutmeg and cloves in a small bowl. Add chicken to spice mixture; toss to coat well.

Heat oil in a 10 inch skillet. Add chicken and onion; cook over medium high heat until chicken is no longer pink. Remove from skillet. Chill mixture in refrigerator until cool.

To the cooled chicken mixture, add ham, pineapple, tomato and sour cream. Toss to mix well.

Serves 2

Cook's notes from Bev and John
Line plates with red leaf lettuce and red bell pepper strips.
Scoop Jerk Chicken Salad in center of plates to serve.

Lobster Salad, What's Cooking? Style

Fresh lobster salad in its extravagant simplicity is perfect for those days when excess seems to be just enough!

Ingredients:

1 1/2 pounds fresh cooked lobster meat
(about three 1 1/2 pound whole lobsters), cut into large chunks
1/2 cup celery hearts, diced
1 shallot, finely chopped
Romaine lettuce leaves

Vodka Dressing:

1 1/2 cups mayonnaise (forget the lowfat versions here!)
1/4 cup sour cream
3/4 cup red chili sauce
1/4 teaspoon red pepper sauce
1 Tablespoon steak sauce
1 Tablespoon finely chopped fresh chives
1/2 teaspoon ground white pepper
1/3 cup vodka

Whisk together mayonnaise, sour cream, chili sauce, red pepper sauce, steak sauce, chives, white pepper and vodka in a bowl until well combined. Cover and refrigerate several hours or overnight to allow flavors to blend.

When ready to serve, combine lobster, celery and shallots with enough dressing to moisten well. Serve on a plate of romaine lettuce leaves.

Serves 1 (or 4)

Cook's notes from Bev and John
Love that Vodka Dressing? Try it as an unbelievable shrimp dip at your next party.

Tarragon Chicken Salad, Too!

This main event will delight your senses with all its tastes and textures.

Ingredients:

6 ounces farfalle (bow tie) pasta, cooked

2 cups cubed, cooked chicken

1/2 cup sliced celery

11 ounce can mandarin orange segments,
drained and patted dry

1 Tablespoon cider vinegar

1 cup mayonnaise

zest of **1** orange

1 teaspoon Dijon mustard

3 teaspoons chopped fresh tarragon
or **1 teaspoon** dried tarragon, crumbled

2 kiwi fruit, peeled and chopped

In a serving bowl, combine pasta, chicken, celery and mandarin orange segments.

In a small bowl, combine vinegar, mayonnaise, orange zest, mustard and tarragon.
Pour dressing over chicken mixture; gently toss to combine. Cover and refrigerate
at least 1 hour up to overnight to blend flavors.

Just before serving, gently mix in kiwi.

Serves 4

Smoked Turkey Salad

All you need to go with this is champagne and someone to do the dishes!

Ingredients:

1 1/2 Tablespoons unsalted butter

2 Tablespoons finely chopped shallots

1 1/2 Tablespoons chopped fresh thyme or **1 1/4 teaspoons** dried thyme

2 cups fresh red raspberries, divided

1/2 cup raspberry vinegar

2 1/4 cups chicken broth

2 Tablespoons Dijon mustard

2 Tablespoons honey

1/3 cup walnut oil

4 Tablespoons champagne vinegar

8 to 10 cups mixed salad greens

1 1/4 pounds smoked turkey, cut into strips

1 1/4 cups coarsely chopped walnuts, toasted

Melt butter in a 9 inch skillet over medium heat. Add shallot and thyme and sauté until shallot is tender.

Add 1 cup of the red raspberries and raspberry vinegar to skillet. Boil until reduced to a thick glaze, stirring frequently, about 7+ minutes.

Add broth and boil until liquid is reduced to 1/2 cup, about 15 to 20 minutes. Whisk in mustard and honey.

Whisk walnut oil and champagne vinegar in a large bowl. Add greens, turkey, remaining 1 cup of red raspberries and walnuts; toss gently to combine.

Pour warm dressing from skillet over salad.

Serves 4

Cook's notes from Bev and John

If you're new to reductions, don't be afraid to stop the cooking process and actually measure to see how you're doing.

Smoked Salmon and Tortellini Salad

Ingredients:

1/4 cup sour cream

1/4 cup plus **1 Tablespoon** extra virgin olive oil

3 Tablespoons fresh lemon juice

2 Tablespoons Dijon mustard

1 Tablespoon dry white wine

1/4 teaspoon ground white pepper

3/4 pound fresh cheese tortellini, cooked

1/2 cup thinly sliced red onion

1/4 cup chopped fresh chives

1/4 cup chopped fresh dill

2 Tablespoons capers, drained

4 ounces smoked salmon, cut into thin strips

In a small bowl, whisk together sour cream, 1/4 cup olive oil, lemon juice, mustard, wine and white pepper. Cover and chill dressing until ready to use.

Transfer tortellini to serving bowl. Add remaining 1 Tablespoon olive oil to tortellini; toss to coat.

Add red onion, chives, dill and capers, stirring gently to blend.

Add salmon and enough dressing to coat and toss well.

Serves 4 to 6

A *Toss* of Steak, Beans and Pasta

Ingredients:

1/2 pound green beans, cooked

1 pound beef flank steak

1 large red bell pepper, cut into chunks

2 large celery stalks, thinly sliced

1 Tablespoon freshly grated ginger

8 ounces of pasta, penne or elbow, cooked

1/3 cup extra virgin olive oil

1/2 teaspoon salt, divided

15 ounce can light red kidney beans, rinsed and drained

3 Tablespoons soy sauce

3 Tablespoons cider vinegar

1 teaspoon sugar

1/2 teaspoon hot pepper sauce

Slice flank steak (across grain) into 1/8 inch thick slices.

In a saucepan (5 to 7 quart) over medium-high heat, cook ginger in hot oil until lightly browned, stirring occasionally. Discard ginger.

In oil remaining in saucepan, cook red pepper, celery and 1/4 teaspoon salt over medium-high heat until vegetables are crisp tender, stirring frequently.

With slotted spoon, remove vegetables to bowl with green beans.

In oil remaining in saucepan over high heat, cook flank steak, stirring constantly until meat loses its pink color and is tender (tasting is the only way to tell if the meat is tender!). Remove from heat.

Return cooked vegetables to saucepan. Add pasta, kidney beans, soy sauce, vinegar, sugar, hot pepper sauce and remaining 1/4 teaspoon salt. Toss to mix well.

Serves 4 to 6

salads

Deli Pasta Salad

Ingredients:

1/3 cup extra virgin olive oil

3 Tablespoons red wine vinegar

1 teaspoon salt

1/2 teaspoon dried basil

1/4 teaspoon hot pepper sauce

1 clove garlic, pressed

6 ounces linguine, broken into thirds then cooked

2 cups cooked roast beef strips

1 cup sliced celery

12 cherry tomatoes, halved

1 cup sliced zucchini

4 ounces fresh mushrooms, sliced

In a bowl, whisk together the oil, vinegar, salt, basil, hot pepper sauce and garlic.

In a serving bowl, combine cooked linguine, roast beef strips, celery, cherry tomato halves, zucchini and mushrooms. Pour dressing over salad; toss gently.

Cover and refrigerate several hours or overnight to blend flavors.

Serves 6 to 8

Curried Chicken Salad, What's Cooking? Style

This salad is rich and spectacular on its own.

Ingredients:

1 1/4 cups mayonnaise

1/4 cup cider vinegar

1 teaspoon ground black pepper

1 clove garlic, pressed

1/2 teaspoon sugar

1/2 teaspoon turmeric

1/4 teaspoon cinnamon

1/4 teaspoon freshly ground nutmeg

1/4 teaspoon dry mustard

1/4 teaspoon cardamom

1/4 teaspoon ground ginger

1/4 teaspoon ground cloves

1/8 teaspoon cumin

1/4 teaspoon cayenne pepper

5 to 6 split chicken breasts, poached then skinned, boned and cubed

1 1/4 cups sliced celery, 1/4 inch thick

2 to 3 cups cubed fresh pineapple

1/2 cup golden or dark, seedless raisins

3/4 cup salted, roasted macadamia nuts

romaine lettuce leaves

Combine mayonnaise, vinegar, black pepper, garlic, sugar, turmeric, cinnamon, nutmeg, mustard, cardamom, ginger, cloves, cumin and cayenne pepper in a large bowl. Blend well.

In a serving bowl, combine chicken, celery, raisins and nuts. Add enough dressing to coat salad ingredients. Add pineapple and serve atop lettuce leaves.

(If you were wondering when you were going to use all those spices in your well stocked pantry, the time is now.)

Serves 4 to 6

Cook's notes from Bev and John
Add the pineapple just before serving to keep it from turning the chicken mushy and making the dressing runny.

Chorizo, Artichoke and Three Bean *Salad*

There's a lot going on in this salad - spicy sausages, delicate artichokes and fresh garlic, onion and jalapenos for flavor, plus a zesty Tomato-Thyme Vinaigrette dressing.

Salad:

2 fresh chorizos, sliced 1/4 inch thick

8 ounce can cranberry or pink beans, drained and briefly rinsed

8 ounce can garbanzo beans, drained and briefly rinsed

8 ounce can black soy beans, drained and briefly rinsed

3 scallions, thinly sliced

1 small red onion, finely diced

2 cloves garlic, pressed

2 small jalapeno peppers, seeded and finely diced

6 ounce jar marinated artichoke hearts, drained and quartered

1/4 cup Tomato-Thyme Vinaigrette

1 Tablespoon chopped cilantro leaves

sea salt and freshly ground black pepper to taste

Brown chorizos over medium heat in a skillet. Drain on paper towels and set aside to cool.

In a large serving bowl, combine beans, scallions, onion, garlic, jalapenos, artichoke hearts and chorizos. Add the vinaigrette and toss well to coat evenly. Add the cilantro and season with salt and pepper.

Refrigerate, covered, for at least half an hour or up to 4 hours to let the flavors blend. Serve chilled or at room temperature.

Makes 8 to 10 servings

Cook's notes from Bev and John

Chorizo is a spicy sausage used in Spanish and Caribbean cooking, made of pork meat and fat flavored with garlic and spices.

Tomato-Thyme Vinaigrette:

1 cup extra virgin olive oil

3 ripe plum tomatoes, cored and quartered lengthwise

1 clove garlic, pressed

1/2 teaspoon chopped fresh thyme leaves

1 teaspoon chipotle purée

1/4 cup balsamic vinegar or more to taste

Heat oil in a skillet over medium-high heat. Add the tomatoes and cook, stirring, until softened.
Add the garlic, thyme, chipotle purée and vinegar and cook, stirring for 2 more minutes.

Let cool. Transfer to a blender or food processor and process until smooth.

Use immediately or cover tightly and refrigerate up to one week. Whisk or shake well before serving.

Makes 1 1/2 cups

Cook's notes from Bev and John
Make chipotle purée from a can of
chipotle peppers in adobo sauce.

Tuscan *Bread* Salad with Tomatoes, Onions, and Olives

If you're a stranger to bread salads, you will be delighted to discover this.

Simply heavenly, bread salads easily lend themselves to whatever variations strike your fancy.

Use excellent, country style bread that is at least a day old, adding enough vinaigrette to evenly moisten the bread…then, do as those in Tuscany do and let the season, your garden and your pantry be your inspiration.

Ingredients:

3 Tablespoons red wine vinegar

Juice of **1** lemon

1 teaspoon Dijon mustard

2 cloves garlic, pressed

2/3 cup extra virgin olive oil

sea salt

freshly ground black pepper

4 cups day old bread cut into 1 inch cubes

2 to 2 1/2 cups cherry tomatoes

1 cup diced red onion

3 Tablespoons finely chopped fresh parsley

1/2 cup pitted Kalamata olives, sliced

fresh salad greens

Combine the vinegar, lemon juice, mustard and garlic. Whisk in the olive oil. Taste the dressing and season it with sea salt and several turns of black pepper.

In a mixing bowl, toss together the bread and most of the dressing, reserving remaining dressing. Let bread sit for 30 minutes.

To serve, add the tomatoes, onion, parsley and olives to the bread and lightly toss together. Add remaining dressing, tossing and tasting the mixture to correct seasoning with salt and pepper as necessary.

Serve bread salad atop salad greens.

Makes 4+ servings

"Meatless" *Taco* Salad

Ingredients:

4 cups frozen corn kernels, thawed, or fresh off the cob

1 small jicama, peeled and cut into small cubes

15 ounce can black soybeans, rinsed and drained

1 red bell pepper, diced

1/2 bunch fresh cilantro, chopped

1 medium head Romaine lettuce, shredded

Taco "Meat":

1 medium onion, diced

1 1/2 pounds soy meat (frozen crumbles)

15 ounce can diced tomatoes

1 teaspoon diced canned chilies

1 teaspoon ground cumin

1 teaspoon chili powder

2 cloves garlic, pressed

1/4 cup finely chopped onion

large bag tortilla chips

Chili Lime Dressing

In a large bowl, combine corn, jicama, black soybeans, red pepper and cilantro. Cover and refrigerate until ready to assemble.

In a large nonstick skillet, cook 1 medium onion, diced, over low heat until tender, stirring occasionally. Add soy meat. Stir in tomatoes with liquid, chilies, cumin, chili powder, garlic and additional onion.

Cook, stirring occasionally, for 10 minutes. Remove from heat.

Add 4 Tablespoons Chili Lime Dressing to Romaine and toss to coat. Pour some of the remaining dressing over the corn/black bean mixture, tossing to blend. To serve: line plates with some of the Romaine, top with corn/black bean mixture then some of the taco meat in the center of the plate. Serve with tortilla chips on the side.

Makes 6 servings

Chili Lime Dressing:

1 cup tamari

1 cup mirin

1/2 cup brown rice vinegar

2/3 cup lime juice

1/4 cup finely chopped onion

1 teaspoon lime zest

1 teaspoon chili powder

In a large bowl, whisk together all ingredients.

Makes 2 1/2 cups

Side Selections

- Fresh Fruit Salad Dressing

- Mixed Greens with Creamy Raspberry Dressing

- Red Skin Potato Salad with Vinaigrette

- Grand Fresh Fruit Bowl

- Wild Toasted Pecan Pilaf

- Mushroom, Sun Dried Tomato and Asparagus Risotto

- Fried Rice with Vegetables

- Shiitake Mushroom, Tomato and Rice Salad

- Pecan Couscous Salad with Zest

- Cinnamon Couscous

- Quinoa Pilaf with Vegetables

- Parmesan Baked Eggplant

- Zucchini Gratinéed

- Bev's Green Bean Salad

- Pine Nut Pilaf

- Tuscan Warm Greens with Balsamic Vinaigrette

127

Words to Eat By

The Romans had a saying when they wanted something done quickly.
"Do it," they said, "in less time than it takes to cook asparagus."
— *Alexandre Dumas*

Lettuce is like conversation: it must be fresh and crisp, and so sparkling that you scarcely notice the bitter in it.
— *Charles Dudley Warner*

Imagination is more important than knowledge.
— *Albert Einstein*

Life is like an onion.
You peel it off one layer at a time;
And sometimes you weep.
— *Carl Sandburg*

Pepper is small in quantity and great in virtue.
— *Pluto*

What small potatoes we all are, compared with what we might be, We don't plow deep enough, for one thing.
— *Charles Dudley Warner*

There are some things that sound too funny to eat – guacamole. That sounds like something you yell when you're on fire.
— *George Carlin*

There's nothing like a good pea!
— *Greg Perrone*

Notes from Bev

John talks: satisfying sides to us are many things – a great salad dressing over your favorite combination of greens, a rice or couscous dish, potatoes provencal, or Bev's family favorite (the Hungarian side) cabbage and noodles.

The common thread is a complement to an entrée – a completion of the meal.

As always, the quality of the ingredients is a prime factor – from the very best wedge of Parmigiano Reggiano cheese that you have grated yourself and possibly frozen for everyday use, to a "just picked" cabbage right out of the local farmer's market garden.

In our "Fundamentals of Cooking" classes one of the first things we teach students is how easy incredibly tasty salad dressings are to make … and what a noticeable difference in taste. Make them and store in your refrigerator for a quick salad or use for an easy marinade.

Noodles, rice and couscous dishes are also simple to make – have the ingredients on hand when that hunger for a super side dish strikes.

The most common question asked in our classes is "What would you recommend I serve with this entrée?" Here they are, some flexible and tasty sides.

Enjoy them!

Fresh *Fruit* Salad Dressing

Ingredients:

1/2 cup sugar

1 1/2 Tablespoons cornstarch or arrowroot

1/2 cup unsweetened pineapple juice

zest of **1** lemon, finely chopped

zest of **1** orange, finely chopped

2 Tablespoons fresh lemon juice

2 Tablespoons fresh orange juice

Combine sugar and cornstarch/arrowroot in a 1 1/2 quart saucepan. Add pineapple juice, whisking until well combined.

Cook, stirring constantly, until mixture thickens and boils. Boil and stir one minute. Remove from heat and add zests and juices, stirring to blend.

Cool until ready to use.

Serve atop fresh seasonal fruit pieces; especially good with pears and apples, as the citrus juices prevent excessive browning.

Makes about 1 1/4 cups

Mixed *Greens* with Creamy Raspberry Dressing

Dressing:

1/3 cup corn or safflower oil

2 Tablespoons sugar

2 Tablespoons raspberry vinegar

1 Tablespoon sour cream or plain yogurt

1 1/2 teaspoons Dijon mustard

Combine all dressing ingredients, blending well with a whisk. Cover and refrigerate until ready to use.

Mixed greens:

4 cups of assorted greens (Romaine, red leaf lettuce, radicchio are just a few choices)

1/2 cup edible flowers (optional)

8 1/2 ounce jar artichoke hearts, drained and chopped

1 pint fresh red raspberries

1 pint fresh blackberries

Combine lettuce and artichokes with blackberries in a large salad bowl. Drizzle dressing on top; toss gently to combine.

Serve topped with red raspberries and edible flowers, if using.

Serves 4+

Red Skin *Potato* Salad with Vinaigrette

Ingredients:

6 to 8 small red skin potatoes

2 medium tomatoes cut into wedges

1/2 red onion, sliced

1/4 cup sliced scallions

1/4 cup pine nuts

1/4 cup safflower oil

3 Tablespoons extra virgin olive oil

2 Tablespoons cider vinegar

2 Tablespoons finely chopped fresh tarragon

1/2 teaspoon salt

1/4 teaspoon freshly ground black pepper

In a 3-quart saucepan combine potatoes and 3 cups boiling water.
Reduce heat; cover and simmer 10 to 15 minutes or until tender.
Drain; cool slightly.

In a large bowl combine tomatoes, red onion, scallions and pine nuts; toss gently.

Combine safflower oil, olive oil, vinegar, tarragon, salt and pepper. Cut warm potatoes
into quarters; place in bowl and top with dressing. Add tomato mixture and toss to coat.
Serve immediately.

Serves 4 to 6

Grand Fresh *Fruit* Bowl

Ingredients:

3/4 cup honey
1/3 cup fresh lime juice
1/4 cup Grand Marnier liqueur
1/8 cup freshly squeezed orange juice

In a 11/2 quart saucepan combine honey and 1/3 cup water. Bring to a boil; reduce heat and simmer 5 minutes.

Stir in lime juice, Grand Marnier and orange juice. Cool completely.

In a large serving bowl, combine fruit as the following suggests: honeydew cubed, cantaloupe cubed, watermelon cubed, nectarines or peaches sliced, fresh blackberries. Pour marinade over fruit; gently mix.

Cover; refrigerate 1 to 2 hours to blend flavors.

Serves 4+

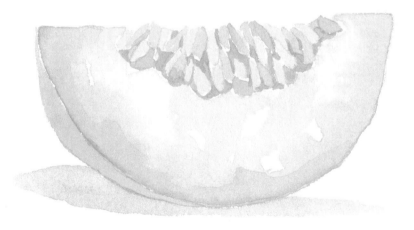

Wild *Toasted* Pecan Pilaf

Ingredients:

1/2 cup coarsely chopped pecan pieces, toasted

1 small onion, halved lengthwise and thinly sliced

1 small yellow bell pepper, cut into thin strips

1/8 cup extra virgin olive oil

1 1/4 cups wild rice, rinsed then drained

1 Tablespoon unsalted butter, melted

1/2 teaspoon dried thyme

1/8 teaspoon salt

2 1/4 cups chicken broth

In a 1-quart saucepan bring broth to a boil. Meanwhile, in an ovenproof casserole cook the onion and the bell pepper in the oil over medium heat, stirring until they are just softened. With a slotted spoon transfer them to a bowl.

Add the rice, butter, thyme and salt to the casserole and cook, stirring constantly, for 1 minute. Stir in broth, adding additional salt and pepper to taste if desired; bring the mixture to a boil.

Bake the mixture, covered, in the middle of the oven for 40 minutes. Stir in the onion mixture, then bake the pilaf, covered, for 30 minutes or until the rice is tender and the broth has been absorbed. Remove from the oven; stir in the pecans and serve.

Serves 4+

Cook's notes from Bev and John
We prefer the taste of hand harvested wild rice ...
look for it when you shop.

Mushroom, Sun-Dried Tomato and Asparagus *Risotto*

Ingredients:

1 Tablespoon extra virgin olive oil

1 large onion, finely chopped

1 leek, halved and thinly sliced

1 clove garlic, pressed

2 cups arborio rice

1/2 teaspoon freshly ground black pepper

8 cups chicken or vegetable broth

20 sun-dried tomatoes, julienned

1 1/2 cups asparagus, sliced into 1/2 inch pieces

1 1/2 cups sliced mushrooms

1/2 cup chopped fresh basil

1/2 cup shredded Gruyere or Swiss cheese

In 5-quart stockpot heat olive oil. Sauté onion, leek and garlic until onion is tender.
Add rice and pepper and sauté for an additional 4 minutes.

In a 2-quart saucepan, heat broth and basil to a simmer.

Add broth mixture, one cup at a time, to rice mixture. Stir often and cook until liquid is absorbed.
Add another cup of broth mixture, repeating process and stirring until liquid is absorbed.

When broth in saucepan is reduced by half, add mushrooms, tomatoes and asparagus to pot.
Stir in to rice as part of the cup of broth.

Cook until mixture is creamy, liquid is absorbed and rice is cooked. Remove from heat and add cheese.

Serves 4+

Fried *Rice* with Vegetables

Ingredients:

3 Tablespoons peanut oil

8 cloves garlic, quartered

2 cups coarsely chopped kale,
preferably Tuscan or Lacinato kale

1 cup oyster mushrooms

4 cups cooked Jasmine rice, chilled

2 tomatoes, seeded and cut into
small pieces

4 teaspoons soy sauce

4 teaspoons fish sauce

1 teaspoon sugar

1/2 cup cilantro, chopped

freshly ground white pepper

Set a wok over high heat. When hot, add the oil and swirl to coat. Add the garlic and stir-fry until lightly browned; remove garlic from wok.

Add the kale and mushrooms and stir-fry until the mushrooms begin to soften. Add the rice, breaking it apart with your fingers as you toss it in.

Stir-fry the rice for 2 minutes, scooping and tossing with a spatula. Add the tomatoes, soy sauce, fish sauce and sugar. Stir well and cook for another 2 to 4 minutes.

Spoon the fried rice onto a platter or plates and sprinkle lightly with the cilantro and white pepper.

Serves 4+

sides

Shiitake Mushroom, Tomato and *Rice* Salad

Ingredients:

1 cup canola, corn or safflower oil

2/3 cup lemon juice

1 Tablespoon Dijon mustard

2 teaspoons dill weed

zest of **1** lemon, finely chopped

2 cloves garlic, pressed

1/2 teaspoon salt

1/4 teaspoon sweet Hungarian paprika

1/2 teaspoon freshly ground black pepper

3 cups hot cooked rice

1/2 pound shiitake mushrooms, sliced

4 plum tomatoes, cut into wedges

4 slices cooked bacon, crumbled

1/3 cup sliced scallions

red leaf lettuce, cleaned and torn into bite-size pieces

Whisk together the oil, lemon juice, Dijon mustard, dill weed, zest, garlic, salt, paprika and pepper in a bowl. Set aside until ready to use.

Toss rice with half of the dressing. Stir in mushrooms and tomato wedges. Cover and chill at least 2 hours or overnight.

Stir in bacon and scallions. Arrange lettuce in a large salad bowl; pour some of the remaining dressing on top. Spoon the rice mixture on top of the lettuce.

Serves 4 to 6

Pecan Couscous Salad with Zest

Ingredients:

2 cups chicken broth

2 Tablespoons unsalted butter

1 1/2 cups couscous

2 cups chopped pecans, toasted

1/2 cup dried cherries or cranberries

zest of **1** orange, finely chopped

zest of **1** lemon, finely chopped

1/4 cup chopped fresh parsley

2 cups mandarin oranges, well drained

1/3 cup fresh orange juice

3 Tablespoons fresh lemon juice

1/4 cup extra virgin olive oil

In a 4-quart saucepan, bring broth and butter to a boil; stir in couscous. Remove saucepan from heat; cover and let stand 5 minutes. Fluff couscous gently with a fork.

In a large bowl, stir together pecans, cherries or cranberries, zest, couscous and parsley.

Add orange juice, lemon juice, oranges and oil and toss salad gently.

Serves 2 to 4

sides

Cinnamon Couscous

Ingredients:

1/3 cup canola oil

3 teaspoons ground cinnamon

2 1/2 cups chicken broth

1 1/4 cups couscous

3/4 cup seedless raisins, golden or otherwise

3 Tablespoons finely minced shallots

2 Tablespoons white wine or champagne vinegar

5 Tablespoons chopped fresh mint (spearmint preferred)

Bring oil and cinnamon to a boil in a 1-quart saucepan, whisking mixture constantly to blend. Set aside to cool.

Bring broth to a boil in a 3-quart saucepan. Mix in couscous and raisins. Cover; remove from heat and let stand 5 minutes.

Transfer couscous to a bowl; fluff with a fork. Cool.

Sauté shallot in small nonstick skillet until golden. Whisk shallot and vinegar into oil mixture. Pour over couscous; add mint.

Serve cold or at room temperature.

Serves 2 to 4

Quinoa Pilaf with Vegetables

Ingredients:

1 cup quinoa, rinsed for 5 minutes under cold running water and drained

1 3/4 cups chicken broth

2 teaspoons extra virgin olive oil

1/2 cup finely chopped red bell pepper

1/2 cup finely chopped yellow bell pepper

1 leek, finely chopped

2 cups finely diced carrots

1/2 cup finely diced celery

2 cloves garlic, pressed

2 Tablespoons freshly grated Parmesan cheese

1/2 teaspoon freshly ground black pepper

1/4 cup chopped fresh parsley

In a 3-quart saucepan, combine the quinoa and chicken broth and bring to a boil.

Reduce heat to low, cover and simmer until the quinoa is cooked and tender and all the liquid has been absorbed, about 15 minutes.

In a 12 inch skillet heat the oil; add the bell pepper, leeks, carrots and celery and cook, stirring occasionally, just until softened.

Stir in the garlic and cook for 1 minute longer. Remove from the heat.

Add the vegetables to the quinoa. Stir in the cheese, black pepper and parsley.

Serves 2 to 4

Cook's notes from Bev and John
This supergrain is pronounced keen wah.

Parmesan Baked Eggplant

Ingredients:

1 eggplant (about 1 1/2 pounds)

salt

3 large eggs

3 Tablespoons milk or water

8 Tablespoons freshly grated Parmesan cheese

2/3 cup dry breadcrumbs

4 Tablespoons finely chopped parsley

2/3 cup unbleached, all purpose flour

1/2 teaspoon freshly ground white pepper

Peel eggplant, if desired; cut into slices. Sprinkle salt on both sides of slices. Let eggplant stand for 30 minutes (this removes bitterness). Rinse with water and pat dry.

Heat oven to 400F.

In a pie pan or shallow bowl, beat eggs and milk. In another pie pan, combine cheese, breadcrumbs and parsley. Place flour and pepper in a third pie pan.

Dust each eggplant slice with flour mixture, dip in egg mixture to coat all over, and then dredge in cheese/crumb mixture.

Line baking pan with parchment or waxed paper. Arrange eggplant slices in a single layer atop paper.

Bake, uncovered, in a 400F oven for 12 minutes. Remove from heat and turn eggplant slices over. Bake an additional 12 minutes or until golden brown.

Serves 2 to 4

Cook's notes from Bev and John
John says, "Yes, definitely peel the eggplant!"

Zucchini Gratinéed sides

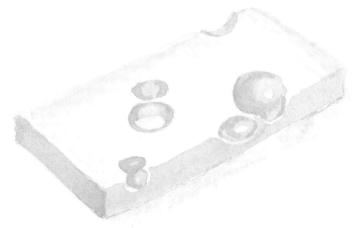

Ingredients:

1/2 cup long grain rice

1/4 cup extra virgin olive oil, divided

2 medium size onions, sliced

1 1/2 pounds zucchini, thinly sliced

2 large eggs

1/2 cup grated Swiss cheese, divided

1/2 cup grated Parmesan cheese, divided

2 cloves garlic, pressed

2 Tablespoons finely chopped fresh parsley

1/2 teaspoon salt

1/2 teaspoon freshly ground black pepper

Bring 1 quart water to a boil in a 2 to 3 quart saucepan. Add the rice and simmer, uncovered, for 15 minutes. Drain in a colander; set aside in a large bowl.

Heat 2 Tablespoons of the oil over medium-low heat in a 12 inch frying pan. Add the onions and cook, stirring occasionally, until very soft. Add to the rice.

Heat the remaining 2 Tablespoons of the oil in the frying pan; increase the heat to medium high. Add the zucchini and cook until wilted.

Add to the bowl with the rice and onions. Lightly whisk the eggs and add them to the bowl with 1/4 cup of the cheeses, the garlic, the parsley, salt and pepper.

Heat the oven to 375F. Lightly grease an 8x10 inch casserole dish. Turn the zucchini mixture into the dish, smoothing the top. Sprinkle with the remaining cheeses and bake for 15 minutes. Increase oven heat to 450F and continue baking for about 10 minutes until the gratinéed is lightly browned and set.

Serve hot or at room temperature.

Serves 4

Bev's Green *Bean* Salad

Ingredients:

2 pounds green beans, trimmed

1/4 cup finely minced shallots

3 Tablespoons balsamic vinegar

1/4 cup extra virgin olive oil

1 teaspoon sugar

2/3 cup chopped fresh basil leaves

1/2 cup grated Parmesan cheese

freshly ground black pepper

Cook beans in an 8-quart stockpot of rapidly boiling water just until crisp tender. Rinse with cold water; drain. Transfer to a serving bowl.

Combine shallots, vinegar and sugar. Whisk in oil.

Add basil to bowl with green beans. Add enough dressing to beans and basil to coat. Gently mix in Parmesan cheese and freshly ground black pepper.

Serves 4+

Cook's notes from Bev and John
Leftovers? Cover and refrigerate. Delicious served cold!

Pine Nut *Pilaf*

Ingredients:

3 cups chicken broth

1 1/2 cups long grain white rice, uncooked

3 Tablespoons unsalted butter

1/2 cup pine nuts

3 Tablespoons chopped fresh parsley

zest of **1** lemon, finely chopped

zest of **1** orange, finely chopped

3 Tablespoons lemon juice

Bring chicken broth to a boil in a 3-quart saucepan; add rice. Cover and simmer for 25 minutes.

While rice is cooking, melt butter in a 1-quart saucepan over low heat. Toast pine nuts in butter until golden brown. Stir in parsley, lemon and orange zests, and lemon juice.

Combine pine nut mixture with rice; stir gently to coat.

Serves 4+

sides

Tuscan Warm Greens with Balsamic Vinaigrette

Vinaigrette:

1/4 cup balsamic vinegar

1/4 teaspoon sweet paprika

1 clove garlic, pressed

1 teaspoon honey

1/4 cup extra virgin olive oil

1/4 teaspoon salt

Salad:

1 1/2 cups sliced white button mushrooms

2 to 3 cups Tuscan or Lacinato kale, cleaned and torn into bite-size pieces

2 cups assorted greens or baby spinach, torn into bite-size pieces

3 Tablespoons pine nuts, toasted

Combine vinaigrette ingredients.

Heat vinaigrette to boiling in a large skillet or sauté pan over medium heat.

Cook mushrooms in Vinaigrette for 3 minutes.

Add kale; toss and cook until greens just begin to wilt. Toss in remaining greens, stirring gently just to coat.

Serve immediately topped with pine nuts.

Makes 2+ servings

Cook's notes from Bev and John
Toast pine nuts quickly in a small nonstick skillet until lightly golden.

Ethnic Favorites

- Hungarian Cucumber Salad

- Budapest Chicken Breasts

- Italian Meat Sauce

- Italian Green Bean Salad

- Jerk Chicken

- Thai Ginger Dressing

- Noodle Cakes with Stir Fried Beef and Tomatoes

- Thai Basil Beef

- Mexican Corn Soup

- Chilies Rellenos Casserole

- Tex Mex Grilled Shrimp

ethnic

Words to Eat By

The trouble with eating Italian food is that five or six days later you're hungry again.
— *George Miller*

… Hungarian housewives and cooks are either born with or develop a keen soup sense.
— *George Lang*

In Mexico we have a word for sushi: bait.
— *Jose Simon*

Notes from Bev

This country's diverse ethnic mix has truly turned us into a global kitchen. Distinct and diverse foods from around the world are available as ingredients, as prepared meals, and as recipes to cook and enjoy.

This chapter offers you a tempting taste of some of our ethnic favorites – from the simplest Hungarian Cucumber Salad to a more time-consuming Italian Meat Sauce. Bev grew up in a home with a Hungarian Mom and an Italian Dad. There was always something cooking: holiday baking traditions, dinner celebrations, picnics, irresistible smells and tastes.

Many of these recipes have passed through our families for generations and, hopefully, they will become your ethnic favorites, too.

Step into our global kitchen!

Hungarian Cucumber Salad

Simple and refreshing describes this Hungarian specialty.

Ingredients:

2 large cucumbers

1 Tablespoon salt

1/4 cup white vinegar

1/4 teaspoon freshly ground black pepper

1/4 teaspoon sweet Hungarian paprika

1 small onion, sliced

Peel and slice cucumbers in paper thin, round slices. Place into a large bowl. Sprinkle with salt and let stand for 30 minutes.

Remove cucumbers from bowl, a little at a time, and squeeze the excess moisture out of the cucumbers. Place squeezed cucumber slices in another serving bowl. Add vinegar, black pepper, paprika and onion. Mix well.

Cover and refrigerate 1 to 2 hours to allow flavors to blend. Serve chilled.

Serves 2 to 4

Budapest Chicken Breasts
(Baked With Onions, Cheeses And White Wine)

Serve with long grain white rice cooked with 1/2 cup chopped parsley; spoon sauce atop rice.

Ingredients:

2 large sweet onions, thinly sliced

3 Tablespoons unsalted butter, plus more as needed

1/4 pound grated Parmesan cheese

1/4 pound shredded Swiss cheese

1 teaspoon sweet Hungarian paprika

1/2 cup dry breadcrumbs

8 split chicken breasts, skinned and boned

1/4 teaspoon salt

1/2 teaspoon ground white pepper

1/2 cup dry white wine

3/4 cup chicken broth

Cook onions in butter in a covered saucepan over medium-high heat until soft and translucent (about 15 minutes). Do not let them brown. Set aside.

Mix together the cheeses, paprika and bread crumbs. Set aside.

Heat the oven to 350F. Set rack in the upper third of the oven. Coat the inside of a baking pan (at least 2 inches deep and large enough to hold the chicken in a single layer … or use 2 pans) with butter.

Spread half the onions in an even layer in the bottom of the pan. Arrange chicken in an even layer over the onions.

Spread the remaining onions evenly over the chicken. Sprinkle the cheese and crumb mixture evenly over the onions, covering the surface completely. Dot some butter evenly over the crumbs.

Combine the white wine with the chicken broth and carefully drizzle the mixture over the crumbs to moisten. Bake, uncovered, in the oven for 1 hour. (The top should be nicely browned.)

Reduce the oven temperature to 250F. Continue cooking the chicken for an additional 30 minutes.

To serve, use spatula to lift each serving from the baking pan. Spoon the sauce on top of the rice.

Serves 6 to 8

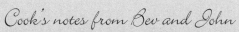

Cook's notes from Bev and John

Assemble and let this dish work wonders ...
as it bakes, it makes its own sauce!

Italian Meat Sauce

That's right, this recipe uses 12 cloves of fresh garlic . . . no vampires tonight!

Ingredients:

1 pound hot or mild Italian sausage, bulk or links with casings removed

1 pound lean ground beef

1 1/2 cups chopped sweet onion

1 cup dry red wine

5 tomatoes, peeled, seeded and chopped

2 ounce can tomato purée

6 ounce can tomato paste

2 teaspoons salt

1 teaspoon ground black pepper

1/2 teaspoon ground fennel seed

1 1/2 Tablespoons dried basil

1 Tablespoon dried oregano

2 bay leaves

12 cloves garlic, pressed

Brown the sausage and ground beef in an 8-quart saucepan, crumbling them as they cook.

When the beef loses most of its color, remove pot from the heat and carefully pour off the fat. Return pot to the heat and stir in the onions. Cook until meat is no longer pink.

Stir in the wine and simmer until the liquid is reduced by half.

Stir in the tomatoes, tomato purée, tomato paste, salt, pepper, fennel, basil, oregano, bay leaves and garlic. Add 1 cup water and simmer the sauce, covered, for 1 hour.

Remove the bay leaves. Serve the sauce immediately or refrigerate for up to 3 days.

Serves 6+

Cook's notes from Bev and John

This is a thick, zesty sauce that is delicious over spaghetti.
Freeze the sauce in serving sizes for up to 3 months.

Italian Green Bean Salad

You could make a meal out of this salad alone! But if you prefer more, serve with a grilled meat and Italian bread for dipping.

Ingredients:

2 pounds green beans, trimmed

3 Tablespoons balsamic vinegar

1 Tablespoon Dijon mustard

1 teaspoon salt

9 Tablespoons extra virgin olive oil

1/4 teaspoon ground black pepper

1 large red onion, peeled, halved and thinly sliced

1 cup pine nuts, toasted

Cook beans in 2 quarts of boiling, salted water until crisp tender. Drain. Rinse under cold water and drain well. Pat dry with paper towels.

Combine vinegar, mustard, salt and pepper in a medium bowl. Slowly whisk in oil in a thin stream.

Combine beans, onion and 1/2 cup of the pine nuts in a large serving bowl. Mix in the vinaigrette. Let marinate, covered, 15 to 30 minutes.

Sprinkle with remaining pine nuts when ready to serve.

Serves 4

Cook's notes from Bev and John
Toast pine nuts in a dry skillet over low heat until fragrant, watching carefully so they don't burn.

Jerk Chicken

Jerk Chicken is uniquely Jamaican, with its key ingredients being Scotch bonnet chili and allspice.

Ingredients:

1 cup finely chopped scallions

3 Scotch bonnet chili, seeded and minced

1 Tablespoon soy sauce

1 Tablespoon fresh lime juice

2 1/2 teaspoons ground allspice

1 1/2 teaspoons dry mustard

1 bay leaf, crumbled

1 clove garlic, pressed

1 1/2 teaspoons salt

1 teaspoon sugar

1 teaspoon peppercorns, crushed

1 teaspoon freshly grated ginger

3/4 teaspoon dried thyme

3/4 teaspoon ground cinnamon

2 1/2 pounds chicken pieces

Make a marinade by blending the scallion, chili, soy, lime juice, allspice, mustard, bay leaf, garlic, salt, sugar, peppercorns, ginger, thyme and cinnamon in a food processor or blender.

Divide the chicken between two heavy-duty plastic bags. Spoon marinade over the chicken, coating well. Seal the bags, pressing out excess air, and let the chicken marinate for <u>at least 24 hours</u> (up to 2 days) in the refrigerator. Turn the bags over several times during marinating.

Brush baking pans with olive oil. Heat oven to 425F. Place chicken, skin side down, in pans. Bake 30 minutes.

Turn chicken, skin side up. Bake 15 more minutes or until done.

Serves 4 to 6

Thai Ginger Dressing

ethnic

A great salad addition to a stir-fry dinner!

Ingredients:

1/4 cup freshly grated ginger

1/4 cup chopped onion

1/4 cup chopped celery

3 Tablespoons white vinegar

3 Tablespoons vegetable (soy) oil

2 Tablespoons lemon zest

2 Tablespoons tomato purée

1/2 teaspoon sugar

salt and pepper to taste

Combine ginger, onion, celery, white vinegar, oil, lemon zest, tomato purée and sugar in a blender. Blend until smooth.

Season dressing with salt and pepper to taste, as desired. Store leftovers in a covered container in the refrigerator.

Cook's notes from Bev and John
Serve this dressing over a salad of shredded iceberg lettuce, red bell pepper strips and enoki mushrooms. Delicious!

Noodle Cakes with Stir-Fried Beef and Tomatoes

Ingredients:

12 ounces beef top round steak,
sliced into bite-size strips

2/3 cup beef broth

1/4 cup soy sauce

2 Tablespoons cornstarch

2 teaspoons white vinegar

1 teaspoon sugar

1/4 teaspoon cayenne pepper

1 Tablespoon vegetable oil

2 cloves garlic, pressed

2 medium green bell peppers cut into thin strips

1 medium onion cut into thin wedges

16 cherry tomatoes, stemmed and halved

Stir together beef broth, soy sauce, cornstarch, vinegar, sugar and cayenne pepper in a small bowl. Set aside. Prepare Noodle Cakes; keep warm.

Heat oil in a wok over medium-high heat. Stir-fry garlic in hot oil for 15 seconds. Add green peppers and onion; stir-fry until vegetables are crisp. Remove vegetables from wok.

Add beef to the hot wok. Stir-fry 2 to 3 minutes or until desired doneness. Push beef from the center of the wok.

Stir sauce. Add sauce to the center of the wok. Cook and stir until thickened and bubbly. Return cooked vegetables to the wok; add cherry tomatoes. Stir, coating well with the sauce. Cover and cook for 1 minute more.

Top each Noodle Cake with beef mixture.

Serves 4 to 6

Noodle Cakes:

8 ounces fine egg noodles

Cook noodles according to package directions until done. Drain and rinse under cold water; drain well.

Make about 16 noodle cakes by placing a generous 1/4 cup cooked noodles for each cake on a greased baking sheet. Shape noodles into patties about 4 inches in diameter. Bake in a 400F oven for 15 minutes or until tops are crisp and lightly browned.

Cook's notes from Bev and John

Noodle cakes, widely used in restaurants, are a creative and tasty vehicle for serving stir-fry recipes – and they're easy to make!

Thai Basil Beef

Ingredients:

2 teaspoons oyster sauce

2 teaspoons soy sauce

2 teaspoons fish sauce (nam pla)

2 teaspoons garlic chili sauce

1 teaspoon sugar

1 teaspoon seeded and minced jalapeno

1 clove garlic, pressed

2 Tablespoons peanut oil

3/4 pound beef flank steak,
cut into thin diagonal slices

1/4 cup beef broth

10 fresh basil leaves left whole

hot cooked rice

Mix oyster sauce, soy sauce, fish sauce, garlic chili sauce, sugar, jalapeno and garlic in a small bowl.

Heat oil in a wok over high heat. Add beef and stir-fry until medium rare. Transfer to bowl using a skimmer.

Pour off all but 1 Tablespoon oil from the wok. Add sauce mixture to wok and bring to a boil. Add beef broth and boil until sauce thickens slightly.

Return beef to sauce in wok. Add basil leaves and stir just until beef is cooked through. Serve over hot cooked rice.

Serves 2 to 3

Mexican Corn Soup ethnic

Ingredients:

1/2 teaspoon cayenne pepper

1 teaspoon cumin

1/4 teaspoon salt

1/4 cup unsalted butter, melted

1 1/2 cups cubed French or Italian bread (1/2 inch cubes)

3 cups corn kernels, thawed and drained if frozen

1/4 cup unsalted butter

2 Tablespoons finely chopped onions

1 1/3 cups half-and-half

2 cups whole milk

1 teaspoon salt

1 teaspoon hot pepper sauce

1/4 teaspoon ground black pepper

1/2 pound Monterey Jack cheese with jalapeno, shredded

Heat oven to 325F. Combine the cayenne, cumin and salt with the butter and toss with the bread cubes until they are well coated. Spread the cubes in a single layer on a baking sheet and bake for 10 to 15 minutes, stirring once halfway through, until golden brown.

Blend the kernels with 1 cup water in a blender to make a coarse purée.

Melt the butter in a 4-quart saucepan. Add the onions and sauté until soft and translucent. Add the corn purée and cook over medium heat for 5 minutes, stirring occasionally.

Add the half-and-half, milk, salt, hot pepper sauce and pepper. Gently heat through, but do not allow to boil.

To serve, ladle soup into bowls. Sprinkle each serving with some of the cheese. Garnish with croutons.

Serves 3 to 4

Chilies Rellenos Casserole

This is an adaptation of a classic that's easy to assemble and not fried.

Ingredients:

4 4 ounce cans whole green chili peppers, rinsed and drained

1 cup shredded sharp cheddar cheese

1 cup shredded Monterey Jack cheese

4 large eggs, beaten

12 ounce can evaporated skim milk

2 Tablespoons unbleached, all purpose flour

1/2 teaspoon salt

1 clove garlic, pressed

1/2 teaspoon cumin

1/2 teaspoon ground black pepper

1/4 teaspoon crushed red pepper flakes

flour tortillas

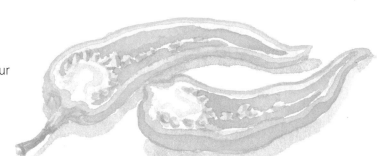

Heat oven to 350F. Grease a 2-quart rectangular baking dish. Pat the drained peppers with paper towels, then halve the peppers lengthwise.

Place half of the chili peppers in the bottom of the dish. Sprinkle with half of both cheeses. Place remaining chili peppers in the dish; sprinkle with the remaining cheeses.

Combine eggs, milk, flour, salt, garlic, cumin and black pepper; beat until smooth. Pour over chilies and cheese; sprinkle with crushed red pepper flakes.

Bake, uncovered, for 30 to 35 minutes or until set in the center.

Stack tortillas, sprinkle lightly with water, then wrap in foil. Place tortillas in oven to warm and soften during the last 10 minutes of baking time.

Serve casserole with warm tortillas.

Serves 6 to 8

Tex Mex Grilled Shrimp

Ingredients:

4 Tablespoons fresh lime juice

4 Tablespoons tequila

2 Tablespoons vegetable oil

2 jalapeno chilies, seeded and finely chopped

1 teaspoon salt

1 pound large, uncooked shrimp, peeled and deveined

Tex Mex Sauce:

1 cup bottled chili sauce

1 jalapeno chili, seeded and finely chopped

2 Tablespoons prepared horseradish

2 Tablespoons fresh lime juice

2 Tablespoons tequila

Combine lime juice, tequila, oil, 2 chopped chilies, salt and shrimp in a bowl; toss to combine. Cover and refrigerate 30 minutes to marinate.

Make Tex Mex Sauce by combining ingredients; cover and set aside until ready to serve.

Place shrimp on an oiled grill grid. Grill (indirect) over medium hot coals for 2 to 3 minutes per side, until shrimp are opaque.

Serve with Tex Mex Sauce.

Serves 4 to 6

Cook's notes from Bev and John
No grill? Shrimp can also be broiled, but watch carefully!
And avoid overcooking as shrimp can become
tough, rubbery (and even burnt).

Sweet Things!

- Cranberry Pistachio Biscotti

- Triple Chocolate Biscotti

- Canadian Maple Dipped Cookies

- Buttermilk Pecan Shortcakes

- Almond Yogurt Sauce over Fresh Fruit
  and Angel Food Cake

- Walnut Shortbread Tart

- Sopa

- Chocolate Fettuccine with Whipped Cream
  and Our Smooth and Silky Fudge Sauce

- Smooth and Silky Fudge Sauce

- Waiter, There's A Truffle In My Brownie!

- Tarte Tatin

- Fresh Fruit and Raspberry Sorbet

- Almost None to Very Little Fat
  But It's Delicious Anyway Mocha Cake

- Meringue Brownies

sweets

Too much of a good thing can be wonderful.
— *Mae West*

Adam was but human – this explains it all.
He did not want the apple for the apple's sake;
he wanted it only because it was forbidden.
— *Mark Twain*

A waist is a terrible thing to mind.
— *Ziggy (by Tom Wilson)*

For when we lose twenty pounds, dear
reader... We may be losing the twenty best
pounds we have!
We may be losing the pounds that contain
our genius, our humanity, or love and honesty.
— *Woody Allen*

I refuse to spend my life worrying about
what I eat.
There is not pleasure worth forgoing just for
an extra three years in the geriatric ward.
— *John Mortimer*

Ah, you flavor everything; you are the vanilla
of society.
— *Sydney Smith*

Bring on the dessert. I think I am about to die.
— *Pierette Brillat-Savarin*

No dessert for you tonight; and don't say
I didn't warn you.
— *Moms everywhere*

Notes from Bev

Oh, dessert, you sweet thing ….

Could we have convinced our publisher to place this chapter first? After all, as one of Bev's aprons says, "Eat dessert first, life is uncertain."

What if you're called away from the table and never get to top off your meal with one of our fabulous desserts!?!

The thought makes us shiver – makes us sad – you poor thing.

But, alas, it won't go to waste; we'll eat it.

We could have easily created just a dessert book, once we compiled our favorites, as well as our students' favorites, from our past years of teaching classes …

BUT

This time we have narrowed them down to the WOW! (like the Waiter, There's a Truffle In My Brownie), the just-a-little-bit-tricky (like the Chocolate Fettuccine), and the homey, comfort food type desserts that are still good enough for company (like the Almond Yogurt Sauce).

Nowhere is cooking more of a science than with desserts ….

Our advice to you is to measure accurately and use the very best ingredients. Read the recipe thoroughly before starting – and relax, have fun and enjoy one of our dessert recipes that taste as spectacular as they look!

Cranberry *Pistachio* Biscotti

I've always adored pistachios, and the combination with dried cranberries is sensational. An adaptation of biscotti we tasted on "The Strip" in Pittsburgh.

Ingredients:

1 cup dried cranberries
2 1/2 cups unbleached, all purpose flour
1 cup sugar
1/2 teaspoon baking soda
1/2 teaspoon baking powder
1/2 teaspoon salt
3 large eggs
1 teaspoon vanilla
1 cup natural pistachio nuts, shelled and coarsely chopped
1 large egg combined with **1 Tablespoon** milk

Heat oven to 325F.

Blend the flour, sugar, baking soda, baking powder and the salt in a bowl until combined.
Add the eggs and the vanilla, beating until a dough is formed; stir in the cranberries and the pistachios.

Turn the dough out onto a lightly floured surface, knead it several times and halve it. Working on a parchment paper lined baking sheet, with floured hands, form each piece of dough into a flattish log – 12 inches long and 2 inches wide. Arrange the logs at least 3 inches apart on the sheet and brush them with the egg wash.

Bake the logs in the middle of the oven for 30 minutes; let them cool on the baking sheet on a rack for 10 minutes.

On a cutting board (with a serrated knife) cut the logs crosswise on the diagonal into 3/4 inch thick slices, arrange the biscotti, cut sides down, on the baking sheet and bake them in the 325F oven for 10 to 12 minutes on each side, or until they are pale golden.

Transfer the biscotti to racks to cool and store them in airtight containers.

Makes about 3 dozen

Triple *Chocolate* Biscotti

Ingredients:

1/3 cup unsalted butter

2/3 cup sugar

1/4 cup unsweetened, Dutch process cocoa
(preferably Droste or Valrhona)

2 teaspoons baking powder

2 large eggs

1 3/4 cups unbleached, all purpose flour

4 ounces white chocolate, coarsely chopped (preferably Callebaut or Valrhona)

3 ounces bittersweet chocolate, coarsely chopped (preferably Callebaut or Valrhona)

Beat butter until softened. Add sugar, cocoa powder and baking powder; beat until combined.

Beat in the eggs; then add in as much of the flour as you can. By hand, stir in any remaining flour, chopped white chocolate and chopped bittersweet chocolate.

Divide dough in half. Shape each portion into an 8 to 10 inch log. Place logs about 4 inches apart on a parchment paper lined cookie sheet. Flatten logs slightly until about 2 inches wide.

Bake in a 375F oven for 25 minutes; cool on a cookie sheet on a wire rack for 30 minutes.

On a cutting board (with a serrated knife) cut each log diagonally into 1/2 inch thick slices. Lay slices, cut side down, on an ungreased cookie sheet.

Bake slices in a 325F oven for 8 minutes. Turn slices over; bake for 7 to 9 minutes more or until biscotti are dry and crisp (do not overbake).

Cool thoroughly on a wire rack. Store the biscotti in an airtight container at room temperature.

Makes about 2 dozen

Cook's notes from Bev and John
Biscotti may be frozen in an airtight container
for up to 6 months.

Canadian Maple Dipped Cookies

Served to us at an outstanding little dessert café in Toronto.

Ingredients:

1/2 cup maple sugar

1/2 cup and **1 Tablespoon** unsalted butter, room temperature

1 large egg

1 teaspoon and **1/2 teaspoon** pure maple syrup

1 1/2 cups unbleached, all purpose flour

1 cup sifted confectioners' sugar

4 to 6 teaspoons milk, 2% or whole

3/4 cup finely chopped pecans, toasted

Beat maple sugar, 1/2 cup of the butter, egg and 1 teaspoon of the maple syrup until well blended. Stir in flour; mix well. Cover dough with plastic wrap and refrigerate until firm.

Heat oven to 375F. Shape teaspoonfuls of dough into logs. Place on ungreased cookie sheets. Bake at 375F for 6 to 8 minutes or until lightly browned and edges are set. Immediately remove from cookie sheets; cool.

Beat confectioners' sugar, remaining 1 Tablespoon butter, 4 teaspoons milk and 1/2 teaspoon of the maple syrup. Beat until smooth and of dipping consistency. Dip ends of cookies in frosting. Roll frosted ends in nuts; allow frosting to set atop waxed paper.

Eat immediately (!) or store in a loosely covered container.

Makes 2 1/2 dozen cookies

sweets

Buttermilk *Pecan* Shortcakes

Ingredients:

1 1/2 cups unbleached, all purpose flour

1/3 cup brown sugar

2 1/4 teaspoons baking powder

3/4 teaspoon salt

6 Tablespoons unsalted butter

3/4 cup toasted pecans, finely chopped

1 cup buttermilk

3/4 teaspoon vanilla

1/4 cup maple sugar

berry assortment of: strawberries, blueberries and red raspberries

Combine berries and maple sugar in a large bowl. Mix gently. Let stand, covered, at least 30 minutes or up to 2 hours ahead:

Heat oven to 375F. Line cookie sheet with parchment paper. Mix flour, sugar, baking powder, baking soda and salt in a food processor. Add butter and pulse until mixture resembles coarse crumbs. Add pecans, pulsing quickly to combine.

Combine 3/4 cup of the buttermilk and vanilla in a large cup. Pulse quickly into dry ingredients, adding additional buttermilk as needed to form fluffy, moist dough.

Scoop dough with a disher onto prepared sheet, spacing 3 inches apart. Sprinkle top of each biscuit with maple sugar. Bake until golden and just firm to the touch, about 15 minutes. Transfer to rack to cool.

Split warm biscuits. Place bottoms on decorative dish. Spoon some berry mixture over each. Top with biscuit tops, spooning more fruit over tops. Serve immediately.

Makes 6 to 8 biscuits

Cook's notes from Bev and John
Of course, serving these with mounds
of freshly whipped cream is also an option.

Almond Yogurt Sauce over Fresh Fruit and Angel Food Cake

Ingredients:

1 cup heavy cream

1/3 cup superfine sugar

1 teaspoon almond extract

1 cup plain yogurt, lowfat or nonfat

3 kiwi

3 plums

2 peaches or nectarines

2 bananas

1 cantaloupe

1 cup blackberries or strawberries

angel food cake

1/2 cup sliced almonds, toasted

Beat heavy cream until soft peaks form. Add superfine sugar and almond extract and continue beating until stiff peaks form. Fold in yogurt.

Spoon almond yogurt sauce into a small bowl; cover and refrigerate until ready to serve.

Cut fruit into wedges. (Pit peaches, plums … peel bananas, cantaloupe and kiwi … we don't really have to tell you that, do we??) Slice angel food cake.

To serve: pass assorted fruit and angel food cake. Pass almond yogurt sauce and toasted almonds to serve atop fruit and cake.

Serves 4+

Cook's notes from Bev and John
Toast almonds in a dry skillet over low heat until fragrant, watching carefully so they don't burn.

167

Walnut Shortbread Tart

Heavenly, easy to make and very rich!

Ingredients:

1/3 cup and **1/4 cup** unsalted butter

1/4 cup sugar

1 large egg yolk

1 cup unbleached, all purpose flour

2 cups coarsely chopped walnuts, toasted

2/3 cup light brown sugar, packed

1/4 cup dark corn syrup or rice syrup

2 Tablespoons heavy cream

Beat 1/3 cup of the butter with the sugar until light and fluffy.
Add egg yolk and beat well. Gradually beat in flour just until blended
(mixture will be crumbly).

Heat oven to 375F. Press dough evenly into bottom and up sides of a 9 inch tart pan with
removable bottom. Bake in center of oven 12 minutes, until lightly browned. Cool on wire rack.

Sprinkle walnuts in bottom of cooled tart shell.

In 3-quart saucepan, stir sugar with remaining 1/4 cup butter, corn syrup and the heavy cream.
Stirring constantly, bring to a boil over medium heat; boil for 1 minute.

Pour over walnuts. Bake tart in center of oven 10 minutes or just until mixture is bubbly.
Place on wire rack to cool. Serve tart at room temperature.

Serves 4+

Cook's notes from Bev and John
Toast walnuts in a dry skillet over low heat until
fragrant, watching carefully so they don't burn.

Sopa

A Spanish-style bread pudding.

Ingredients:

2 cups sugar

6 Tablespoons unsalted butter

1 1/2 teaspoons ground cinnamon

1 teaspoon vanilla

1 pound loaf white bread, toasted and cut into cubes (about 10 cups)

2 cups shredded cheddar cheese

3/4 cup raisins

1/2 cup peanuts

Place the sugar in a 3-quart saucepan. Cook over medium-high heat, without stirring, until sugar starts to melt. Reduce heat to low; cook until sugar is golden brown, stirring frequently. Remove from heat.

Carefully add 2 1/2 cups water (it will splatter). Return saucepan to heat. Bring to boiling, stirring to melt hardened lumps. Remove from heat; stir in butter, cinnamon and vanilla.

In a 3-quart rectangular baking dish, layer half of the bread cubes. Sprinkle half of the cheese and all of the raisins over the bread cubes. Top with the remaining bread cubes, remaining cheese, and nuts. Pour caramelized sugar mixture over all.

Bake, uncovered, in a 350F oven for 30 minutes or until top is golden and syrup is absorbed. Serve Sopa warm.

Serves 4+

Cook's notes from Bev and John
Toast bread slices in a 325F oven just until crisp.

Chocolate *Fettuccine* with Whipped Cream and Our Smooth and Silky Fudge Sauce

Great fun to do ahead in stages and then serve as a spectacularly simple dessert for a dinner party! The Smooth and Silky Fudge Sauce is also delicious spooned directly out of the jar or over ice cream!

Chocolate Crepes (batter for 10 to 14 crepes):

3 large eggs

1/8 teaspoon salt

1 cup milk

1 cup <u>less</u> **2 level Tablespoons** unbleached, all purpose flour

2 Tablespoons clarified butter, melted

2 Tablespoons unsweetened cocoa (preferably Droste or Valrhona), sifted

1 Tablespoon vanilla

1 Tablespoon sugar

1 cup heavy cream

In a blender or food processor, combine eggs, salt, milk, flour, melted butter, cocoa, vanilla and sugar. Process to combine, stopping and scraping bowl as needed, until smooth and well mixed.

Pour mixture into bowl and cover bowl with plastic wrap. Let batter rest at room temperature for 2 to 3 hours or up to 12 hours in the refrigerator. (This step is very important – it enables the flour to expand and absorb the liquid. A batter that has rested will work much better than one that's freshly made.)

Cook's notes from Bev and John
Confused by clarified butter?
Refer to page 179 for information and instructions.

Brush the inside of the crepe or 7 inch omelet pan with a small amount of the clarified butter. Heat the pan over medium high heat. Pour 1/4 cup of the batter into the hot pan, swirling quickly to cover the pan bottom.

Cook on one side until the edges are lightly browned. Flip (using a metal spatula to carefully lift and your fingers to lift and flip) and cook for 15 additional seconds. Repeat until all batter is used. Let crepes cool. Cover if holding for later use.

To serve: whip 1 cup heavy cream; set aside. Cut each crepe into long strands about 1/4 inch wide with a very sharp knife. Separate the strands and toss them lightly with your fingers so that they resemble fettuccine noodles. Place them in a large pasta bowl.

Spoon the whipped cream mixture into the center of the pasta bowl. Toss the "fettuccine" with the whipped cream. Serve with our Smooth and Silky Fudge Sauce.

Serves 4+

Cook's notes from Bev and John
When making and stacking the crepes, put a
piece of wax paper between each cooked crepe
to prevent them from sticking together.

Smooth and Silky *Fudge* Sauce

Ingredients:

4 ounces bittersweet chocolate, chopped into pieces
(preferably Callebaut or Valrhona)

1/3 cup unsalted butter

1 1/3 cups confectioners' sugar, sifted

5 ounce can evaporated milk or 3/4 cup half-and-half

1 teaspoon vanilla

Combine the chocolate, butter, sugar and milk or half-and-half in a 3-quart saucepan, mixing well. Cook, stirring constantly, over medium heat until mixture boils.

Reduce heat to low. Cook 5 minutes, stirring constantly. Remove from heat; stir in vanilla.

Store any leftovers (!!??) in a covered container in the refrigerator.

Makes about 2 cups

Waiter, There's a *Truffle* In My Brownie!

An all-adult version you'll soon be addicted to.

Ingredients:

1/2 cup unsalted butter

3 ounces bittersweet chocolate, cut into chunks (preferably Callebaut or Valrhona)

1 1/3 cups sugar

2 large eggs

1 teaspoon vanilla

1/2 cup unbleached, all purpose flour

1 pound (more or less after eating a few on the way home!) chocolate truffles, your choice of flavors with solid centers, cut into 1/2 inch pieces

Heat oven to 350F.

Combine the butter and bittersweet chocolate in a double boiler set over simmering water. Stir often over low heat until chocolate/butter is melted and smooth.

Remove from heat; transfer to a bowl. Beat in sugar, eggs and vanilla, blending well.

Stir in flour and truffle pieces. Pour into lightly buttered 9 inch square pan. Bake until brownie is just set, about 25 to 35 minutes. (Do not overbake; brownie will firm up more as it cools.) Let cool in pan on a wire rack.

Serve warm or cool, cut into pieces. Top portions to taste with vanilla ice cream or frozen yogurt and a sprinkling of cocoa powder.

Serves 1 to 6!

sweets

Tarte *Tatin*

A lightened version of a classic - we've used our basic dough rolling and chilling technique to make handling of fragile dough easier for you.

Ingredients:

1 cup cake flour, sifted

1/2 cup plus **3 Tablespoons** sugar

3 Tablespoons unsalted butter

5 medium Golden Delicious apples, peeled, cored and sliced into 8 pieces

1 Tablespoon lemon juice

3 Tablespoons maple sugar or brown sugar

1/4 cup plus **2 Tablespoons** vanilla yogurt, lowfat or nonfat

1 Tablespoon sour cream, regular, lowfat or nonfat

Combine flour and 2 Tablespoons of the sugar in a bowl; cut in butter until mixture resembles coarse crumbs.

Sprinkle 2 Tablespoons of ice water, a little at a time, over crumbs tossing until mixture holds together lightly. Press mixture into a disc shape on plastic wrap, cover with additional plastic wrap, and chill 20 minutes.

Combine apples, 1 Tablespoon of the sugar and lemon juice in a bowl; toss well. Let stand 15 minutes.

Roll covered dough to an 11 inch circle. Place in freezer for 10 minutes.

Sprinkle remaining 1/2 cup sugar in a 10 inch ovenproof skillet and place over medium heat. Caramelize by stirring often until sugar melts and is golden (about 8+ minutes).

Add apple mixture and cook just until apples are tender; do not stir. Remove skillet from heat.

Remove plastic wrap from dough. Place dough on top of apples in skillet, gently tucking dough around inside edge of skillet. Cut 4 to 6 slits in dough for steam to escape.

Bake at 425F for 20 minutes or until browned. Invert onto serving platter.

Combine maple sugar, yogurt and sour cream; stir well. Drizzle as a glaze over warm tart.

Serves 4+

Fresh Fruit and *Raspberry* Sorbet

This is an easy to make sorbet with an intense raspberry flavor.

Ingredients:

1 envelope unflavored gelatin

2 10 ounce packages frozen red raspberries with syrup, thawed

1/2 cup light corn syrup

1/3 cup Chambord

3 Tablespoons lemon juice

1/4 teaspoon salt

an assortment of fresh fruit, such as kiwi, mango, blood oranges and fresh raspberries

In a 1-quart saucepan sprinkle gelatin over 1 cup water; let stand 1 minute to soften gelatin. Cook over medium heat, stirring, until gelatin completely dissolves; set aside.

In a food processor blend raspberries with their syrup, one package at a time, until puréed. Press puréed raspberries through a sieve into a large bowl to remove seeds.

Stir corn syrup, Chambord, lemon juice, salt and gelatin mixture into raspberry juice. Pour mixture into 9x9 inch baking pan.

Cover pan with foil and freeze, stirring occasionally to evenly distribute frozen edges, until entire mixture is partially frozen, about 3 hours.

Spoon raspberry mixture into chilled large bowl. With electric mixer beat at medium speed until smooth but still frozen, scraping bowl occasionally with rubber spatula. Return mixture to pan; cover and freeze until firm.

When ready to serve, arrange scoops of sorbet into individual dessert dishes with some fresh fruit.

Serves 4 to 8

sweets

Almost None to Very Little Fat But It's Delicious Anyway *Mocha* Cake

This is our son, Ray's favorite cake . . . once you've enjoyed it, you'll understand why.

Ingredients:

1 cup unbleached, all purpose flour

1/3 cup unsweetened cocoa
(preferably Droste or Valrhona), sifted

1 1/2 teaspoons instant espresso powder

1 teaspoon baking powder

1 teaspoon baking soda

6 large egg whites

1 1/3 cups light brown sugar

1 cup coffee yogurt, lowfat or nonfat

1 teaspoon vanilla

Topping:

1 1/2 teaspoons confectioners' sugar, sifted

1 teaspoon ground cinnamon

1 teaspoon unsweetened cocoa, sifted

Heat oven to 350F. Line bottom of a 9 inch round cake pan with parchment paper.
Lightly grease parchment paper and sides of pan; dust with sifted cocoa powder, tapping out excess.

Sift flour, 1/3 cup of the cocoa, espresso powder, baking powder and baking soda into a bowl.
Beat egg whites, brown sugar, yogurt and vanilla until blended; add dry ingredients.

Pour batter into cake pan. Bake for 35 minutes or until cake tester or toothpick inserted in center comes out clean. Cool in pan on rack 25 minutes.

Cut around pan sides to loosen cake. Turn cake upside down onto rack; peel off parchment paper and invert cake onto rack; cool completely.

Sift confectioners' sugar, cinnamon and the remaining cocoa in a small bowl. Sprinkle over cake and serve.

Serves 4 to 8

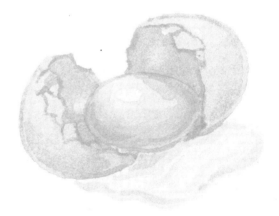

Meringue Brownies

Ingredients:

1/2 cup unsalted butter

1/4 cup unsweetened cocoa powder, sifted (preferably Droste or Valrhona)

3/4 cup unbleached, all purpose flour

1 teaspoon baking powder

1 cup sugar, divided

1 1/2 teaspoons vanilla, divided

1 teaspoon chocolate extract (pure, not imitation)

3 large egg whites, room temperature, divided

1/8 teaspoon salt

Melt butter in a 1 1/2 quart saucepan over medium heat. Whisk in cocoa, until smooth. Pour mixture into a large bowl.

Add flour, baking powder, 3/4 cup of the sugar, 1 teaspoon of the vanilla, chocolate extract and 2 of the egg whites to the bowl. Stir well to blend.

Spread batter into a nonstick 9 inch square baking pan.

Beat remaining egg white with salt until foamy. Gradually add remaining 1/4 cup of the sugar, a little at a time, beating until stiff peaks form. Fold in remaining 1/2 teaspoon vanilla.

Spoon egg white mixture on top of batter; gently and quickly spread meringue topping with a thin metal spatula.

Bake at 325F for 25 minutes or until meringue is set and lightly browned. Cool completely in pan on a wire rack.

Makes about 1 dozen brownies

Glossary of Terms and Ingredients

Arrowroot: The starchy product of a tropical tuber of the same name. The rootstalks are dried and ground into a very fine powder. Its thickening power is about twice that of wheat flour. Arrowroot is absolutely tasteless and becomes clear when cooked. Unlike cornstarch, it doesn't impart a chalky taste when undercooked.

Bread Flour: An unbleached, specially formulated, high gluten blend of 99.8 percent hard wheat flour. It is ideally suited for yeast breads.

Blind Baking: An English term for baking a pastry shell before it is filled. The shell is usually pricked all over with a fork to prevent it from blistering and rising. Line shell with foil then fill with dried beans or rice. The beans/rice and foil should be carefully removed a few minutes before the baking time is over to allow the crust to dry and brown evenly.

Balsamic Vinegar: Gets its dark color and pungent sweetness from aging in barrels over a period of years.

Cream (to): To beat an ingredient or combination of ingredients until the mixture is soft, smooth and "creamy." Often a recipe calls for creaming a fat, such as a butter, or creaming a mixture of butter and sugar.

Cooking Wine: Not to be used in cooking, not to be purchased, not to be used in anything. If the wine you're using isn't good enough to drink, don't cook with it!

Caper: The flower bud of a bush native to the Mediterranean and parts of Asia. The small buds are picked, sun dried and then pickled in vinegar brine. Capers are generally packed in brine but can also be found salted and sold in bulk.

Clarified Butter: A process of melting unsalted butter in a heavy pan over low heat keeping it from browning; the white froth that rises to the top is skimmed off with a spoon and the clean yellow "clarified" liquid butter should be carefully poured off into a container, leaving the white curdlike dregs in the pan to be discarded. Allows foods to be cooked at higher temperatures and for longer without the butter blackening and becoming acrid.

Direct Method: (Not to be confused with ways to pick up people at bars.) In grilling, food is placed on a grid directly above the hot coals. The grill can be open or covered. Direct heat is most often used for cuts of beef, which cook in a relatively short period of time such as steaks, burgers or kabobs.

Deglaze: To dissolve in the pan with wine, stock or other liquid the sediment left in the pan after the meat, poultry or fish has been cooked in a small amount of fat.

Elbow Grease: Using your arm to do more stirring, kneading or whisking than you would like to – don't be such a baby! It's good therapy!

Fold (to): A technique used to gently combine a light, airy mixture (such as beaten egg whites) with a heavier mixture (such as whipped cream or custard). The lighter mixture is placed on top of the heavier one in a large bowl. Starting at the back of the bowl, a rubber spatula or whisk is used to cut down vertically through the two mixtures, across the bottom of the bowl, and up the nearest side. The bowl is rotated a quarter turn with each series of strokes. This down-across-up-and-over motion gently turns the mixtures over on top of each other, combining them in the process.

Fines Herbes: A mixture of chopped herbs such as parsley, chervil, tarragon and chives used to flavor omelets, salads, chops and more.

Five Spice Powder: Seasoning used in Chinese cuisine. Available at Asian markets, this easy to make-it-yourself mixture can be used in any recipe calling for five spice flavor: 1 teaspoon cinnamon, 1 teaspoon crushed anise seed or star anise ground, 1/4 teaspoon crushed fennel seed, 1/4 teaspoon fresh ground black or Szechwan pepper, 1/8 teaspoon ground cloves. Combine well and store tightly in a covered container.

Hot Spots: Found on cookware of poor craftsmanship; refers to areas of cookware where food has a tendency to burn.

Indirect Method: In grilling, foods are cooked by reflective heat, similar to the way in which conventional oven cooks. Procedure: open or remove the grill cover. Open the bottom dampers. Arrange a number of briquettes on each side of the fire grate. Ignite the briquettes and burn until ash covered. Make certain coals are burning equally on both sides; it may be necessary to move hot coals (with long handled tongs) from one side to the other to have heat evenly distributed. Place disposable aluminum drip pan between sets of coals. Depending on the size of your grill, the number of charcoal briquettes required for each side can range from 15 to 30. For gas grills: refer to your manufacturer's instructions for indirect grilling. Usually it's a matter of leaving one burner off to cook over with the lid closed and a drip pan under that area of the grill (to catch any dripping and thus avoiding flare-ups). Be sure to discard drip pan when done grilling.

Knead: A technique used to mix and work a dough in order to form it into a cohesive, pliable mass. During kneading, the network of gluten strands stretches and expands, thereby enabling a dough to hold in the gas bubbles formed by a leavener (which allows it to rise). Kneading is accomplished either manually or by machine. Well kneaded dough is smooth and elastic.

Leek: Looking like a giant scallion, the leek is related to both the garlic and the onion, though its flavor and fragrance are milder and more subtle. It has a thick, white stalk that's cylindrical in shape and has a slightly bulbous root end. Choose those with crisp, brightly colored leaves and an unblemished white portion. Avoid any with withered or yellow spotted leaves. Trim rootlets and leaf ends. Slit the leeks from top to bottom and wash thoroughly to remove all the dirt trapped between the leaf layers.

Panade: A sweet or savory soup made with breadcrumbs and various other ingredients. It may be strained before serving.

Parchment Paper: A heavy, grease and moisture resistant paper with a number of culinary uses including lining baking sheets, wrapping foods that are to be baked "en pappillote" and to make disposable pastry bags.

Pine Nuts: Also called Indian nut, pinon, pignoli and pignolia this high fat nut comes from several varieties of pine trees. The nuts are actually inside the pinecone, which generally must be heated to facilitate their removal. This labor-intensive process is what makes these nuts so expensive.

Peeling Tomatoes: Drop tomato into a pot of boiling water, cooking for 30 seconds to 1 minute. Immediately remove tomato and place into a bowl of ice water. When cool enough to handle, skin should easily slip off with fingers or a sharp paring knife.

Proof (to): To dissolve yeast in a warm liquid (usually with a small amount of sugar) and set it aside in a warm place for 5 to 10 minutes until it swells and becomes bubbly. This technique proves that the yeast is alive and active and therefore capable of leavening bread or other baked goods.

Rice Wine: Distilled from fermented rice and made in many varieties, qualities and strengths; sake, sherry or dry vermouth can be substituted for rice wine in cooking.

Sweat (to): A technique by which ingredients, particularly vegetables, are cooked in a small amount of fat over low heat. Traditionally, the ingredients are covered directly with a piece of foil or parchment paper, then the pot is tightly covered. With this method, the ingredients soften without browning and cook in their own juices.

Superfine Sugar: Known in Britain as castor sugar, superfine is more finely granulated than traditional white sugar. Because it dissolves almost instantly, superfine sugar is perfect for making meringues and sweetening cold liquids. It can be substituted for regular granulated sugar cup for cup.

Scant: A little less than full, i.e. a scant teaspoon.

Sesame Oil: Expressed from sesame seed, sesame oil comes in two basic types. One is light in color and flavor and has a deliciously nutty nuance. The darker, Asian sesame oil has a much stronger flavor and fragrance and is used as a flavor accent for some Asian dishes. Sesame oil is high in polyunsaturated fats ranking fourth behind safflower, soybean and corn oil. Its average smoking point is 420F, making it excellent for frying.

Sauté: To cook food quickly in butter or other hot fat, stirring to brown it evenly.

Sate/Satay: In Indonesian cooking, pieces of meat or seafood marinated in a spicy sauce, skewered and grilled. Usually served with a peanut sauce.

Zest: The perfumy outermost skin layer of citrus fruit (usually oranges or lemons) which is removed with the aid of a zester or Microplane, paring knife or vegetable peeler. Only the colored portion of the skin (and not the white pith) is considered the zest. The aromatic oils in citrus zest are what add so much flavor to food.

Several words on ingredients: We always use the "best ingredients available," cooking with the seasons, and if we know a certain product works best for a recipe or has a much better flavor we recommend it.

Some of our cooking *preferences* and *prejudices*:

Butter: We always use unsalted or sweet butter in baking and cooking. Why butter? It enhances the flavor and texture of the dish. Remember, moderation is the key to good health.

Cooking Wine: When a dry red or white wine is called for use a moderately priced wine that's drinkable, not one labeled "cooking wine" – too bitter and vinegary!

Carrots: Whenever you can, buy unpeeled fresh carrots with the green tops still on. (And you thought carrots grew in plastic bags!)

Chicken Breasts: If possible, skin and bone yourself (as soon as they have been skinned and boned they begin to dry out and lose flavor). Again, maximize tenderness!

Flour Unbleached, all-purpose flour is our absolute favorite (more specifically, Montana Sapphire, Bob's Red Mill or King Arthur brands). They are purer and in some recipes, such as crusts, work the best.

Garlic: Use fresh bulbs and break off cloves as needed. We like to press it in a garlic press, which allows you to not have to peel off the skin from the cloves.

Lemon Juice: Use fresh, not "Real Lemon" product; a suitable substitute is Minute Maid frozen lemon juice and/or Santa Cruz Organic lemon juice, both pure.

Maple Syrup: Use pure and local. Forget that the imitation maple syrup even exists.

Olive Oil: In general, use a flavorful, fruity (green) moderately priced extra virgin olive oil (to your own taste) for cooking and a cold pressed, extra virgin olive oil (golden) for bread dipping and salads. Buy several, taste and pick your favorites.

Parmesan Cheese (and other hard cheeses): Buy a fresh wedge of cheese and grate it yourself. Use Parmigiano Reggiano for ultimate flavor.

Peppercorns: Grind your own for freshness and flavor. We prefer tellicherry black peppercorns – a great bite!

Parsley: Use flat leaf, Italian parsley as an ingredient. It is less bitter and therefore will give your dishes a better flavor. Save the curly parsley for garnish!

Shrimp: Shell and devein your own shrimp, cook it only until just cooked through, and it will be tender and flavorful. We prefer "white" shrimp over "tiger" shrimp – more flavor.

Vanilla: Make your own! Buy a 375 ml bottle of 80 proof, moderately priced vodka (such as Smirnoff). Cut two vanilla beans in half and place all four pieces of vanilla beans into the bottle of vodka. Label and let steep in a cool place (out of direct sunlight) for 4+ weeks or until the vanilla smells right. You will see little flecks of vanilla floating in the vodka. Do not be alarmed; this is a great thing! Also, you will notice that your "vanilla" does not become excessively dark – that's because there's no coloring in it. It's pure and natural. Our preference for type of vanilla bean is Madagascar Bourbon beans for maximum flavor. This makes a wonderful gift for someone who loves to bake.

List of *Recipes*